Simple Wealth

By

Andrew Costello

Copyright © 2011 by Andrew Costello (All rights reserved).
SIMPLE WEALTH and SIMPLE WEALTH: BUILDING WEALTH
FROM SCRATCH registered trademarks of Andrew Costello.

INTRODUCTION

This book was written for one reason and one reason only. To make you wealthy!

There is no other reason to read it.

It is here to teach you how to build up your wealth from scratch. Starting with absolutely nothing, as I did, and ending up with more than you could ever imagine.

Having wasted many years learning individual techniques from different sources, and having had much of my precious time (and money) wasted by "motivational speakers", "guru's" and "financial advisors", I have collated everything you need to know about wealth into one brief tome.

A little guide book that you can follow easily and without any further cost.

There are no expensive courses to attend and no CD's or DVD's to buy. And I can assure you that there certainly won't be any $2000 per ticket seminars. That small amount you already paid for this book is all you will ever have to spend.

Why?

Because you're not going to get wealthy by giving all your money to someone else, are you?

If you are willing to follow the formula that I will teach you, and learn to make good use of your short time on this planet, you will know riches that most men can only dream of!

If not, you may as well close the book now. You'll be poor forever.

> *"This is the path to wealth. Let the wise man follow it"*

THE AUTHOR

Right now, if you're smart, you'll be wondering what gives me the right to try and teach you about becoming wealthy. What are my credentials?

The answer is very simple.

My growing wealth does! My bank account, my assets and my lifestyle are my credentials.

WHO TAUGHT ME?

I myself learned most of these techniques from another book called "The Richest man in Babylon". It changed my life! From that point on, I have dedicated myself to learning about wealth, and how to acquire the most of it that I can.

I have moved from being absolutely powerless, to having almost total control over my life. I have gone from being broke, to having enough money to get me through any situation.

I have used this formula for more than 10 years now.
And in that time, I have gone from being a pathetic loser, who was stone-broke, destitute and heavily in debt, to being completely debt free, and having enough money that I don't have to worry about it anymore.

I am finally free to live the life that I want to live.

THE JOURNEY

Along the way, I have learned a lot. And still have a lot more to learn yet.

But the important thing is that I am in control of my own destiny, and I am growing wealthier by the day. I have all the power over my life and decide what I am going to do, and how I'm going to do it.

All thanks to a simple little formula. A formula that anyone can follow!

THE FUTURE

And over the next 10 years, what will I do? I will continue to follow this method, and grow even wealthier because of it. Before that time is up, I shall easily have become a multi-millionaire.

And after that decade has passed?   Who knows? Maybe one day I will even become a billionaire. And yet, I have never possessed a high paying job to speak of or a university degree either.

Items I was always told were essential to becoming rich.

DON'T FALL FOR LIES

I have learned that those "requirements" are a lie, and that wealth doesn't come from your earnings, or your intelligence, or stupid pieces of paper. And it certainly doesn't come from taking expensive courses, or paying for ridiculously overpriced "motivational experts" to cheer you on.

It comes from how hard you work, how you use your money and how you live your life.

> *"That is the one and only true secret to wealth."*

WELCOME TO REALITY

We are waking up to a new world. The Western Empire is dying.

The life that we all knew for so long is rapidly disappearing, as the false wealth of the credit boom evaporates before our very eyes.   It is quickly being replaced by the growing roar of creditors, demanding to know where their money is, and why they have not received repayment yet.

So, just like the end of the roaring twenties, the days of easy money, gained purely by borrowing and spending, are almost over.

But this time, the Western Empire will disappear with them.

As with the fall of previous empires, the aftermath will be terrible, and many will suffer. Vast numbers of people, who previously lived in luxurious comfort, will descend to lives of squalor and hardship. And even the most powerful will tremble as their positions of power slowly erode, to give way to new masters.

But by the end of this book, that will all be completely irrelevant to you.

Because although it may be time for the dying Western Empire to once again join the real world. It is time for you to learn how to become wealthy.

Thankfully, this little book is here to teach you everything you will ever need to know.

It will show you how to develop the type of real and robust wealth that will carry you through any period, and any economy. Giving you the security of being able to put food on the table, no matter what happens, and no matter who is running things.

So you will not only survive these changes that are currently occurring, but will eventually outgrow them altogether. This will lead you to experience a freedom that most men will never know.

The freedom of true wealth!

You might think that this is an overstatement, or perhaps an exaggeration. But this is because, like most people, you have been brainwashed into believing your Empire is invincible and will last forever. And that your government, religion, social class, [insert any other inane institution you happen to belong to] will protect you from harm.

Just like the Sumerians did, and the Egyptians, and the Greeks, and the Persians, and the Romans-…..you get the point. Empires end. All of them!   And this time round it is ours.

But that doesn't mean you have to end with it.

Let's be honest, you want to be wealthy. Otherwise you wouldn't be reading this book.

That's really good. It shows that you are ready to be responsible, as all true men should be. It is just as important as learning to put your children before yourself, and you can be equally proud of it. You have taken that first important step toward embracing your new reality and becoming wealthy.

But first, do you actually know what wealth is?

Most people think they do. When in actual fact, they have no idea. They dream of being given a big pile of money to go shopping with, to buy fancy cars, and beautiful jewelry, and designer clothes. But that is not wealth. That is just spending. It is the fantasy of fools.

> *"A fool and his money are easily parted."*

What makes a wealthy person different is that they have the resources to buy those things. They don't have to borrow money, or be given money, eventually losing everything once the pile runs out. They can pay cash, and keep their purchases forever. And still have plenty more resources in reserve to buy all the other things they want.

And for every dollar they spend, more dollars will appear to replace it.

That is wealth!

There will be many things in this book that you may find offensive. I really don't care.

You'll just have to live with it.

Because this is a guide to building your wealth, not some self-esteem class for the weak and unmotivated. So if you do find yourself offended by any of the lessons and truths that I present to you, just ask yourself one question,

"Are you wealthy?"

If the answer is no, then clearly you are doing something very, very wrong. So it's time to stop taking offense, and to start taking good advice.

This book will help you in ways that you cannot even begin to understand at this stage. But most of the lessons are geared toward absolute beginners, and will benefit you from the very day you start using them.

So sit back, get comfortable, and learn how to make your fortune in the 21st Century.

THE CLOCK IS TICKING!

This is your life. Whether you like it or not! And like all men, it is the only one you will ever get.

You can delude yourself all you like with fantasies of after lives, reincarnation or any other childish rubbish that you wish to indulge in. But you are just wasting your most precious resource. Time!

You will still only get one life. It is not up for negotiation. There are no Gods to bargain with. And more importantly, that single life is finite. It is a non-sustainable resource in its own right. Never to be replenished.

It is all just basic mathematics. Like everything else in the Universe.

TICK TOCK

Whether you like it or not, you have a set amount of time on this planet, and every single minute that goes by means you now have a minute less.

This is something that you should be thinking about as you go about your day.   Because it is the most important thing you will ever know. And once you understand that, you will accomplish far more with the time you have left.

Sadly, most people will foolishly believe that they have more time. That more opportunities will present themselves. But that is just not true. They will wake up one day, bitter, old and full of regret.

"Time waits for no man."

Time is one of the few things you can never get back. No matter what happens.

HOW MUCH TIME DO YOU HAVE?

Nobody can know that for sure. You could get hit by a truck tomorrow. Or have a heart attack at 29. Then again, you could live to a hundred.

All we can create is a very good estimate. So let's arbitrarily make up a life span for you.

If you are under 30, living in a Western nation, which you probably are, your life span will be somewhere around 75. Because you, like most of your friends, are in the first group in more than a century, who will not outlive their parents lifespan. So let's go with that figure.

Do you know how many days that is?

That's 27,375 days! (Not including a few extra days for leap years).

That may seem like a very long time. It usually does when you are young and stupid. But just remember back to when you were 10 years old. Didn't 20 seem like a long time away?

In fact, let's go all the way back to when you were born.

Think about your first week of life. It went by rather quickly, didn't it? So quickly, that you are unable to even remember it. But at the end of that first week, that you no longer remember, you had 27,368 days left to live!

What about the first year? Your parents took care of you. You grew substantially, and probably even started to learn to walk. Maybe you spoke your first word too. But these great achievements are lost to the passage of time as well.

Speaking of which, at that point you had 27, 010 days left.

Most readers will be in your early twenties, because this is an electronic book, which effects the demographic of the audience. In fact, let's say it's your 22nd birthday, just for arguments sake.

You now have 19,345 days left to live.

Almost a third of your life is gone! Yep, almost one third of your time on planet earth is behind you. And once you hit 32 years old?

That's when you should really start to get worried.

Why?

Because your body is beginning to deteriorate! Your muscle mass is degrading, and your brain cells are starting to die off at a more rapid rate than before. And the worst part is, everybody knows it! Which means employers are now roughly 75% less likely to hire you in an unskilled job and the opposite gender is almost 90% less likely to find you attractive!

And by the way, you have 15,695 days to go till you die!

> "Are you starting to understand just how short life is?"

As with milk, your expiration date will come much faster than you thought it would.

At the ripe old age of 50, five decades will have passed in what seems like the blink of an eye. You will be unable to find low skilled work of any kind, because you are too expensive to hire, and are no longer physically capable of a lot of tasks. So you **better** have a skilled career well established! Otherwise, you will not have any income, and no way to gain one.

You will feel tired for no apparent reason. Your eyesight and hearing will start to fade. And a bank will now be more than 70% less likely to give you a mortgage. If you don't own a home by now, there is more than a 95% chance you never will.

What have you done with your life???

9,125 DAYS TO GO!

That's right. At 50 years old, you are only 9,125 days away from your very last breath. Can you believe it's gone so fast?

You started with 27,375! And that doesn't seem like it was very long ago.

TIME SPEEDS UP

Time is running out more rapidly now, as each day seems to speed past. This is because you are slower and cannot do as much as you used too. During the next 25 years, you will have less patience and less tolerance for others.

Superficiality will bore you, and you will yearn for something interesting to happen. You will start to have many regrets.

By 60, your body will not keep up with your mind. And you will discover you cannot stand loud noise and crowds anymore. You hate cities and the problems that come with them. Everything is becoming more confusing. And you don't understand a lot of the new technology that is appearing.

You wish your family would spend more time with you.

You are getting old.

BANG! YOU'RE OUT OF TIME

Those last 25 years have now passed. You wake up realizing you are 75 years old. Your time has expired.

If you are lucky, you will get to die in your own bed. If not, you will find yourself in a hospital, surrounded by uncaring, greedy doctors, sick people and despotic nurses.

Despite what you might see in the movies, it is highly unlikely that your family will be there. They are far too absorbed with their own lives.

In most cases, you will take you last breath **alone**. Terribly frightened of what death will be like. And in those last few moments, as you realize that you are dying, you will have just enough time to look back upon your life.

THE QUESTION IS

What will you see?

HOW DO I KNOW THIS?

It's not just pretentious ramblings, or a wild guess. I've interviewed many people over the years, in my study of wealth, and most of them were old. And as a soldier, I saw enough people die to know how frightened by it they were.

It is not something to look forward to.

Anyone who glamorizes death doesn't know what the hell they are talking about. Neither does anyone who speaks of gods, heavens and hells. They're just ignorant people talking shit. Pure and simple!

You can learn a lot by talking to old people, or people who are dying of battle wounds. And the reality is that they all told the same story, over and over. Similarities kept popping up. It was actually kind of disturbing in a strange way.

Some were rich and had led full lives, while others were dirt poor, wondering who would pay for their funerals. But they all understood the truth at that stage. They had come to realize that all men are born equal, and that life is what you make of it. Everything else is just an excuse.

Even the ones who had done nothing with their lives admitted that they had had as many chances as the ones who were staggeringly rich. But they had failed to make use of their time and opportunities in the same way.

They admitted that they had failed to take advantage of the things that every person has.

They were bitter, vindictive and full of regrets. But it was all directed at themselves. Not others.

SIMILARITIES WHERE NONE APPEAR TO BE

It's stunning to encounter so many people, from so many back grounds and discover that their origins and nationality had nothing to do with their wealth or poverty. Not a damn thing!

At first glance, I would never have dreamed that they would all have had such similar experiences and opportunities in their lives.

But they had.

They had all grown from babies to old age, and earned a lot of money in between. Some had done a lot with it, others had done nothing. But they had all had the same chances. Most of them had even earned similar amounts in the jobs they had worked.

A man from Africa had grown rich selling herbs and plants, just like a man from my home country of New Zealand.

Another writer from the United States had gone through the same submission difficulties and hardships that I myself had gone through, and even started a T-shirt business to pay his bills in the meantime, just like I did many years ago. And now we both invest in physical silver.

A telecommunications company in Mexico had been just as viable as one in the United States. And a movie star from Brazil had built up her career, just like her new friend from California. They met at an audition, and discovered many commonalities.

And naturally, the poor ones had all taken the same actions too.

A homeless man in Sydney was just as irresponsible as a homeless man I met during my time in the Solomon Islands, and a mother dying of lung cancer in Fiji told the same story as a colleague of my own in Wellington who was suffering from the same disease.

On the face of it, all these people may have appeared different. But once you hear about their lives, you realize that they are exactly the same. We all are.

DENIAL

Personally, it took me quite a while to admit what I had found. Because it nullified all the excuses I'd made in my life. It was hard to accept that we are all the same. That everything was my own fault.

Most people find it difficult to admit that they've messed up their lives. But I think it's even worse when you've turned your life into a disaster zone like I had.

At that time, I was nearing the end of my period of false starts. And I couldn't deny it any longer. I was financially poor because of my own actions, and no other reason.

I had wasted the moderate amounts of wealth that I had created with the formula on "get rich quick schemes". Trying to subvert the very laws of nature in the process, and failing, as all are destined to do when they think they can take a short cut.

Every problem I ever had was my own fault, and my time was running out.

So is yours!

DESPERATION

I admit that my own wealth has been built through desperation and fear. I didn't want to end up like the poor people I had met. In fact, I was absolutely terrified of it.

It was so clear how badly they had wasted their lives, and would receive no more chances. I wanted more than that. Their lives had been completely ***pointless*** in the end.

Even my time in the army getting shot at didn't cause me as much fear as the idea of dying like those people. I would have nightmares about lying in that hospital bed, old and lonely, knowing that there would be no more opportunities. That my time had come to an end!

But I'm glad that I felt so afraid. I'm even proud of it in a way.

It's what spurred me on to follow the formula strictly. From there on in, I had to accept that it was all up to me.

And I did. The question is, will you?

QUESTIONS

Before you can be wealthy, there are two important questions that you must ask.

1. **Why** are people poor?
2. **Why** are people wealthy?

You will get absolutely nowhere without asking these questions, because the answers will give you a much deeper understanding of wealth and how to achieve it.

So that is where we are going to start.

WHY ARE PEOPLE POOR?

WHY ARE PEOPLE POOR?

The very simple truth is:

> *"People are poor, because they **want** to be."*

That may shock you! Or perhaps you are offended, as we previously discussed. It doesn't matter. It is still completely true. And by the end of this book, you will come to see it for yourself.

And the truth shall set you free!

> *"People are poor, because they **want** to be."*

WHAT ABOUT YOU?

If you yourself are poor, or moving toward that state, there are very specific reasons for this.

All of which are completely self-inflicted. And all of which can be easily overcome with enough effort and determination.

Don't believe me? You will by the time we finish.

There are certain habits you have developed, or beliefs that you have adopted, that are making you poor. You are **sabotaging** yourself. Or perhaps, you are allowing *others* to sabotage you. Either way, it needs to stop.

These habits come in many forms. But they are all connected to each other by their destructive, and wealth sapping, nature. Here are a few examples:

1. Using credit instead of cash.
2. Living from paycheck to paycheck.
3. Using drugs (including alcohol and cigarettes)
4. Borrowing for a lifestyle beyond what you earn.
5. Driving a car you cannot afford.
6. Living in a house or apartment that is too expensive.
7. Pretending to be rich, when you are clearly not.
8. Refusing to admit you cannot afford something.

Those are just some of the poverty inducing habits that most people engage in. And if you want to be wealthy, you have to be willing to change, and stop indulging yourself in such stupid (not to mention childish) behavior.

CHANGE IS THE ANSWER!

"Change is the path to all things"

If you are lucky, one day you will truly grasp how important that sentence is.

It took me several years, lying awake at night thinking about it. But I eventually came to understand the enormity of it.

The amount of success you find in life will be directly correlated to the amount you are willing to change. Because at the end of the day, this is all one great big science experiment!

But let's get back to the point, shall we.

WHY WOULD PEOPLE WANT TO BE POOR?

This is a very good question. It seems to go against all logic. But there are many reasons.

Eternal Victims

These are people who are attention seeking, where the "victim" enjoys the attention that comes from telling their "sob stories". It makes them feel important when they aren't anything of the sort, and allows them the attention they crave, but without having to do anything even vaguely useful with their lives.

Lazy Scum

These are truly despicable individuals who have no intention of working, or paying their own way through life. They like to try and make others feel guilty for working hard and being successful. They believe that hard working people should have to share the rewards of their success with the less deserving individuals such as themselves. Their only goal is to make the minimum effort possible in their lives. These people tend towards unions, communism and socialism.

The Fearful & Immature

Some people are just plain scared of wealth, and the responsibility it brings. The very idea of growing up frightens them.

They don't want the hassle of acting like adults, and taking responsibility for their own lives. Preferring to try and hold onto their childhood forever, so someone else has to take responsibility for them. It's called Peter Pan syndrome.

Often, they will rely on things like charity, welfare, religion or some other parental substitute to comfort them, and give them the sense that someone is there to take care of them.

The Selfish

And then, there are others who are just downright selfish. They are not interested in anything except their own hedonistic desires. They could not give a damn about their family, community or country. Not even their children! Their only focus in life is themselves. Nothing else matters to them.

All of these reasons are as pathetic as each other. And in most cases, you'll find people suffer from a combination of them. But they all lead to the same outcome eventually. It's called poverty.

REMEMBER THIS

"If you want to be poor, you will be poor."

WHY ARE PEOPLE WEALTHY?

WHY ARE PEOPLE WEALTHY?

Just like poor people cause their own poverty, in order to feed an ulterior motive or desire, so do wealthy people.

They are wealthy because they want to be wealthy.

They have decided that this is the life they want, and seek ways to live it. And like all things in life, where there is a will, there is a way.   So they eventually find a path to that wealth. One way or another!

That is something that you must understand if you are going to be wealthy. Because, as Henry Ford once said,

> *"Whether you think you can, or think you can't, you're right."*
>
> - Henry Ford

There is no obstacle that cannot be overcome!

PERSONAL ANECDOTE

I learned this myself, when after 11 years of trying I finally got a green card to live in the USA. Something that I had been told would never happen! According to everybody else, it was impossible, because I did not fit into any visa category.

Lawyers told me it would never happen. The State department website told me it would never happen. Family members told me it would never happen, and friends told me it would never happen. They all criticized and mocked me behind my back for many years for continuing to try, whispering that I was a fool and was wasting my time.

But then it did happen!

WHY DID THEY FIND IT IMPOSSIBLE

To them it was impossible, because they were not willing to put much effort in.

But to me it was possible, because I decided not to give up until I possessed one. And sure enough, I was selected in the DV lottery.

Strangely enough, by that stage I was also moving toward the point where I would have enough funds for the investment category as well, and had developed my script writing skills to the point where I would be able to enter under the talent category a year or two later.

I had found several paths to my dream. All of which were apparently **impossible**.

"Wealth is all about wanting it, and being willing to take the actions necessary to get it."

HABITS OF WEALTHY PEOPLE

Just like poor people, wealthy people also develop certain habits and attitudes too. Here are a few of the more important ones.

1. They consistently spend less than they earn.
2. They consider saving an important part of their life.
3. They pay off their debts, and stay out of debt.
4. They pay cash whenever possible.
5. They use coupons, and discount deals.
6. They DO NOT play the big shot, impressing others.
7. They will accept that they cannot afford some things.

Those are just some of the habits, but all are well worth noting and following.

That alone will bring you a lot of wealth over the years to come. You may have to force yourself to do them for the first few months, but then they will become natural, and your brain will come to understand them as a state of normality. After all, that's how habits form. By constant repetition!

REMEMBER THIS

"If you want to be wealthy, you will be wealthy!"

THE FORMULA FOR POVERTY

The causes of poverty are now so well known, that there is even a set formula for achieving it. And like all mathematics and science, this formula is easily testable. And the same results will occur with every test.

Go out and give it a go. Or better yet, just observe a bunch of poor people, and watch how they follow it. Either way, you'll very quickly see how well this formula works.   It is absolutely 100% guaranteed to lead to poverty.

THE FORMULA FOR POVERTY

Here is the basic formula for growing poor.

1.	Spend too much on luxuries.
2.	Borrow to pay for your necessities.
3.	Fail to pay your debts on time.
4.	Save nothing.

This is the guaranteed formula for poverty, and it never fails. If you follow it, you will always end up poor. And the longer you follow it, the harder it will be for you to ever find your way out of that poverty.

Eventually, you will get to the point that you become so used to being poor, that you will believe your poverty to be a permanent state of being, and then you will live like that till the day that you die.

Sadly, **most** people **do** choose to follow this formula.

THE FORMULA FOR WEALTH

Just as there is a formula for poverty, there is also one for wealth.

It is very simple. And anyone who follows it will immediately find their position in life, greatly improved. And over time, their wealth will continue to build until it is an ***unstoppable*** juggernaut.

In fact, the only way to stop getting wealthier is to stop following the formula.

THE BASIC FORMULA FOR WEALTH

A self-made wealthy person spends their money like this:

1. 10% toward their fortune.
2. 20% toward their debts. (Till they are fully paid)
3. 60% toward their necessities.
4. 10% toward enjoying their lives.

If you want to be wealthy, then you too must make your spending look like this.

It is also known as basic mathematics. If you're waiting for it to get more difficult, please don't hold your breath. Because that is all there is to it. It doesn't get any harder than that.

The rest of this book is merely a breakdown of that formula, showing you how, and why, it works.

If you can understand that 10% + 20% + 60% + 10% = 100%, then you are smart enough to become incredibly wealthy. That is all the intelligence required.

SIMPLIFICATION

I will try to expand on this formula, bit by bit throughout this book, to make things easier for you, which is more than anybody ever did for me. I had to work it all out by myself. So count yourself lucky.

SAVINGS

Separate 10% out of every paycheck you earn, and place it in a secure account. Whether it is a regular contribution term deposit, or physical silver, bonds, or a locked savings account doesn't matter. It's your choice. It just has to be something that you are unable to access quickly.

For at the start, most people do not have the will power to resist the temptation to spend their savings. Later on, you will. But right now, you are still a financial weakling. So you have to lock the money away so that you cannot touch it.

Have it done by automatic payment, so you don't even get to see that money. For the first 12 months, you may resent not having access to it. But after a while, you'll find you don't even miss it.

If you can comfortably save more than 10%, then do so. But don't stretch yourself too far.

*TIP
The strange thing about money is that people will spend as much as they have access to. Whether it is $10 or $1000, they will always find ways to go through every single cent of it. And their "expenses" will always rise to the exact amount of money they can get access to.

DEBT

Separate 20% of your income, and place it toward paying off your debts, also by automatic payment. Becoming debt free is one of the most important steps to becoming wealthy. And no debt is insurmountable if paid off in small parts on a regular basis.

If your creditors pressure you for more, explain that they can take what you offer, or take nothing and allow you to default on the debt. As that is all you have.

Believe me when I say that they will not turn the money down. Mainly because they know damn well that the bank just created the money they loaned to you out of thin air.

They never loaned you anything that really existed in the first place. (This is completely true. You can go look it up).

And once those creditors are paid off, never take another debt again!

It will take you many years to repay your debts. It took me more than half a decade. But it is a harsh lesson in why not to buy things you cannot afford.

*TIP
There is a hugely profitable scam in the financial industry, where "debt experts" will tell you to pay your highest interest debts off first.

This is a complete con to get more money out of you as the debts continue to accumulate with interest. Effectively creating a situation where you pay and pay, but the principle never goes down.

They are being paid (very high commissions) by the credit card companies and corporations to tell you this. It helps guarantee that big corporations increase their profits, and their smaller competitors go out of business.

Always contact all your creditors directly and come to an agreement to repay a certain amount each paycheck, in exchange for the account being frozen, and no more interest being added on. Each creditor should get an equal amount each payment. For instance, if you have $50 a week to pay with, and there are 5 creditors, they get $10 each.

THE COST OF LIVING

Separate 60% of your income, and modify your necessities to match it. And do not allow it to account for a single cent more.

Make **NO** excuses, because excuses are for poor people. And remember, your "expenses" will always rise to match the exact amount you have available for spending.

If your rent is too high, ***move***. If your bills are too high, ***reduce*** them. Most of what people consider their necessary expenses are really nothing more than petty wants and desires. Very little of it is actually necessary for you to live.

In the last 10 years, I've yet to encounter any working person whose necessities are actually more than about 40% of their income. And even that seemed to provide a pretty luxurious life.

Yet I've encountered an endless list of people who waste a lot of money on completely useless things they really don't need.

LUXURIES

Separate 10% of your income, and place it toward the enjoyment of life. Because what good is living if you don't have any fun or excitement? Go to movies, have a night out with friends, engage in a hobby or go out for dinner.

Whatever brings you the most personal enjoyment! But be clear, no man should attribute more than 10% of his earnings toward such ventures, because it will lead him to laziness and ruin.

I honestly don't know why this is, but the rule holds true in every single situation.

All the people I've encountered who spent more than 10% of their income on luxuries ended up ruined. It's like some kind of natural self-destruction level. Every cent over the 10% mark ends up going on over consumption, drugs, and other harmful products that wind up destroying the spender.

SIMPLE HABITS

Those are the spending habits of wealthy people. And they should become your spending habits too. It is a very basic formula for wealth that will lead you toward a situation where you are financially free.

If you can spend less in any area, then you will merely grow rich faster. And if you can get out of debt, you can apply the extra 20% to your savings so they will grow stronger. But don't be a fool.

Even the smallest increases in spending on luxuries or the cost of living can result in ruin. This structure has been perfected over 5000 years, and dozens of civilizations. It has been well tested, and proven to be true over that time. You have to trust in the experiences of all those who came before you.

WHERE WILL IT LEAD YOU?

All of you want to be wealthy, but not all of you will be. The people who read this book will fall into 3 categories.

The Weak

Those who are just too addicted to their false wealth, and cannot bring themselves to change. They will make endless excuses, and deny reality, all the while falling further and further behind as each day passes, until they wake up very old men, and realize that it is too late.

The Fools

Those, who like me, will have a few false starts, before realizing how foolish they were and accept their mistakes. They will then go on to follow the formula strictly, cursing themselves for not doing so sooner. They will waste much opportunity and have many regrets.

The Strong

There will also be a few, very smart people, who see the wisdom of this formula and start following it today and never stop. They will be the billionaires of the 21st Century.

I would encourage you to be far smarter than I was, and throw your lot in with the last group. It will save you a lot of wasted time, money and heart ache, because you will accomplish absolutely nothing by delaying your acquisition of wealth. I know this from bitter experience.

PERSONAL ANECDOTE

Throughout the years, every time my wealth stopped building, it was because I stopped following the formula.

I got caught up in false advice, promising instant riches without effort. Or I was listening to "financial advisors" and "gurus". All of whom were out to destroy my wealth for their own gain.

Naturally, they all turned out to be liars. And like clockwork, every time I started following the formula again, my wealth started to grow.

I estimate that I have lost more than a million dollars, purely through this moronic inability to consistently follow simple instructions. And I deeply regret that. As would anyone who realizes they have been a fool.

Had I acted more responsibly and followed the formula strictly from the very first time I learned of it, I would have an extra million dollars sitting in my bank account.

Think about that figure, One Million Dollars. I do!

WHICH FORMULA WILL YOU FOLLOW?

Hopefully, if you're reading this, it is because you do not want to be poor. You want to be different.

Maybe you're young and don't like the idea of working in a degrading, pointless job for the rest of your life. Perhaps you are old, and just want a few years of dignity before you die. Or maybe, like me, you experienced many years of poverty and hated every moment of it. It really doesn't matter.

What matters is that you want to be different.

You want to be wealthy! That one simple little desire puts you ahead of 99.9% of humanity. Because most people just want to spend. They enjoy being poor. In fact, they absolutely love it. And there is no way to wealth for those who don't want to be wealthy.

But for anyone who does want to be wealthy, following the formula for wealth will quickly lead them there.

WHAT WILL THIS BOOK DO FOR YOU?

This book will teach you the formula for wealth.

A formula that leads to a life of plenty, and a life of meaning! And it is through this formula that you will find your way out of debt, and into the warm, loving embrace of wealth.

Of course, it is up to you to decide which formula to follow.

Either way, you'll reach your goal.

THE HISTORY OF WEALTH

Thankfully, over the centuries, many other people have also wanted to be wealthy, and they have worked out the basic method to becoming so. They did this mainly through trial and error. Sorting out what works and what doesn't work.

The first of these were the Babylonians, who recorded it in cuneiform (the beginnings of written language).

Followed by many others in the centuries, and civilizations, that came after them.

Some used eloquent words, while others put it into numbers. But they all taught us the same thing. They gave us a formula that leads straight to wealth.

This formula is specific. It is simple. And most importantly, **anyone** can use it.

WHAT DO YOU HAVE TO DO?

All you have to do is follow the formula they set out. And the rest will come automatically.

It really is that simple. I look back now, and realize that any problems I encountered along the way to my wealth were all completely self-inflicted, and came from not following the formula.

But whenever I went back to following it strictly, the wealth started to build once more without fail.

It really is automatic.

HOW GOOD IS IT?

This method of building real wealth has been tried and tested by so many people, over so many centuries, that no one can deny it works. It is 100% guaranteed.

It has also been mathematically proven by many, many scientists.

So everything you learn here will work, just as it worked for the thousands of generations that came before you. And no doubt, the results will be the same. If you follow it to the word, you will immediately begin building your wealth. And it will only stop building, if you stop following the formula that is set out.

That's how good it is.

It turns out that wealth is simple. It is just a basic mathematical formula. Like everything else in the Universe.

YOUR HISTORY - WILL YOU BE RICH OR POOR?

Whether you choose to be rich or poor is entirely your own decision now. Nobody else can make it for you.

They can only judge you for it in the future.

This book may provide you with all the knowledge you need, but it cannot give you the motivation. That has to come from within. It has to be your own choice. You have to write your own story. This is literally your history in the making!

Because another truth is, the only person in control of your life is you.

> *"Nobody, whether man nor god, decides your fate but you!"*

The only power people have over you is what you allow them to have.

WHAT IF YOU DON'T LIKE YOUR LIFE?

You can walk away at any time and get on with a life you do like, and building your wealth. No matter what the situation may be. No one has any real power over you whatsoever. And to believe differently is the folly of fools.

If you do choose to follow the advice of this book, you will end up with far more than you would ever have had otherwise.

That's something you should **think** very long and hard about.

THE KEY TO WEALTH

Many thousands of years ago, mankind started to realize something.

A family group would move into an area, hunting and gathering what they could. But after a while, there were no more animals to hunt and there was nothing left to gather.

So, they would have to move on again.

But after a while, they also began to run out of areas to move too as well. Or they came into conflict with other family groups who were already there.

They realized that resources are *scarce*.

This very simple realization is the absolute "**KEY**" to wealth. And it is the first thing you need to know to build wealth.

If resources were not scarce, there would be no such thing as wealth. We could all just have whatever we wanted. The world would be a very different place.

Curiously enough, this "**KEY**" is why humanity took the step to becoming farmers and producers. Even the uneducated men of that simple age could see very clearly that if you did not replant foods, they would soon run out. Likewise, if you did not allow the animals to reproduce, you would soon go hungry. In other words, they noticed that resources are scarce.

But unlike most of their kind, they decided to do something about this scarcity. They wanted to have enough resources to carry on, through both good times and bad. They wanted to survive!

In other words, they wanted to be wealthy.

So, humanity (at least some of them – many family groups died out) learned to replace what they used.

They found a secure area near water to live. And they learned to grow enough crops, so that there would always be plenty of fruits and vegetables, and to breed animals for their offspring before the parents were killed and eaten.

This steady supply of food, and the stability and cooperation it brought with it, allowed humanity to carry on.

It also allowed them to think of other ways to improve their lot in life. Such as using less than they had, and to not waste valuable resources, so they could trade their excess with others, for new types of resources, better sexual partners, and security.

"**Conservatism**" was born.

Conservatism is the act of thinking about what you have, and how to ration it in a way that allows you to have some resources, all of the time. Instead of running out during the winter, or other difficult times that may come about.

It was the basis of the early Western Empire, and the beginning of every other empire throughout history as well.

As opposed to "**consumption**", which can be defined as the relentless use of resources to the point of exhaustion, which usually results in the downward spiral of an empire because once the resources run out, the people starve.

Conservatism is the major difference between "Producers" and "Consumers".

PRODUCER (Conservative in nature)

An individual, or group, that takes the future into account, and acts in a responsible manner to ensure that they have enough resources to ensure their survival, and the survival of those who rely upon them.

CONSUMER (Wasteful in nature)

An individual, or group, who think only of the moment, and consume irresponsibly, with no thought of tomorrow, or others.

THE CONSEQUENCES OF CONSERVATISM

And that is why you are here reading this book today.

That one moment of wisdom, to move from wasteful consumers, to conservative producers, meant that some homo-sapiens continued on into the future.

To have descendants who would be born, and live, and have descendants of their own. Some of whom you are probably related too. Their "productive and conservative" genes are likely to be one of the many influencing factors that led you to buy this book.

It's also why some people are NOT reading this book today.

They're ancestors failed to learn these simple lessons, wastefully consuming resources upon sight, and eventually running out of those resources, and so their descendants did not even come into existence.

Will yours?

IT'S NOT ALL ABOUT YOU

You are not just responsible for yourself. But also your children, and grandchildren, and great grandchildren, and so on…. They are all relying on you to get through your lifetime, attaining enough resources in the process, so they can have their chance at life.

RESOURCES ARE SCARCE. THIS IS THE ABSOLUTE KEY TO WEALTH.

 In order to survive, ancient man learned to understand the very simple concept that there are not enough resources for everybody to have as much as they want, and from that, they learned to be conservative and productive. Avoiding waste, and maximizing their output, in order to build up their level of available resources. In other words, they grew wealthy.

And so must you.

That is the whole concept of wealth. Learning to produce and save resources, so that you can survive further into the future, and breed offspring into a better environment, who will also survive to carry on and do the same.

Wealth is primarily about the survival of your DNA. Of course, it has many other benefits too. But it is your DNA that matters.

So this is the first lesson to becoming wealthy in the 21st Century.

> *"Resources are scarce."*

And scarily, as time goes by, they will become even scarcer.

Every single day, the human population of earth increases!

The growth rate is roughly 200,000 people per day. It's a very sad fact. And every single one of those new people consumes some of the resources that are available on the planet we all share.

Some of those resources are non-sustainable, because there is simply a finite amount of that particular resource on the Earth. These cannot be replaced or regrown. We would have to go to other planets to get more.

These include things like silver, copper, oil and other ores that we mine.

Other resources are sustainable. They can be replanted, remade, or even reused. These are things like, fruit, vegetables, paper, animals, cotton, wool etc…..

HOW WILL THIS MAKE YOU WEALTHY?

1. Anyone who produces more sustainable resources than they use, will always grow wealthy by trading their excess.

2. Anyone who produces more non-sustainable resources than they use, will always grow incredibly wealthy by trading their excess.

3. Anyone who consumes more than they produce will always end up in poverty.

These are the three laws that govern resources. They are binding throughout the Universe and will always hold true, the same way the laws of physics hold true. If you try to go against them, you will **fail**.

That works out very well for you! Because most humans consume far more than they produce, and will happily buy any excess that you produce.

SIMPLE RULES OF RESOURCES

1. Production increases your wealth.
2. Consumption decreases your wealth.
3. Excess can be invested or traded.

How easy is that?

It is just simple addition and subtraction. The more you produce, the wealthier you will become. The more you consume, the poorer you will become. This is basic math, and will always hold true. No matter what the context.

So you need to find some kind of sustainable system, where your production is higher than you consumption.

Producing more than you consume quickly leads to wealth, because that is how nature works. Like all things, it is a mathematical equation.

"That knowledge alone can bring you great wealth."

HOW CAN YOU APPLY THAT KNOWLEDGE?

Clearly, you have to produce more resources than you consume, and trade the excess for other types of resources you don't produce.

So essentially, you need to think about what you are, or could, be good at producing.

Whether it be growing potatoes in your yard, painting houses, building engines, drawing for comic books, baking pies, mowing lawns or manual labor. You must find something that you can apply your energy toward to produce an outcome.

Then you must concentrate all your efforts on it to increase your productivity in that field, and become as good as you can in your chosen skill, increasing the level of quantity and quality as you do so.

For those without business experience, it's a good bet that people will always need food, shelter and clothing. And these are the easiest resources to produce. So starting with sustainable resources is your best bet in the short term, with an eye to moving into non-sustainable resources in the long term.

Although, having said that, there are many families who have stayed rich for several generations purely through sustainable resources like food, or clothing. Their wealth has only ended when a generation has lost the urge to be wealthy, and gone back to consuming more than they produce.

PRODUCTION VERSUS CONSUMPTION

If you're having any trouble thinking about this concept, and many do, you may need to look at it in practical form. Rip a piece of paper up into 10 pieces and pretend they are resources (in this case, wages).

Give 5 to your landlord (5 left). Give 3 to utilities providers (2 left). Spend 2 on food (0 left).

Give.......oops. There are no more to give. They quickly disappear, don't they?

Now, take the 10 pieces back. This time we'll do it differently:

Give 4 pieces to your mortgage provider (6 left). Take 3 pieces from a boarder (9 left). Give 2 pieces to your utilities providers (7 left). Take 1 piece for selling home-made jam (8 left). Spend 2 on food (6 left). Take 2 for interest on a term deposit (8 left).

Are you starting to get the picture? In this scenario, you are producing more than you consume.

In the first scenario, you quickly go broke. But in the second, you have all the things that the first person has, and still have a lot of resources left to buy more. And all through very small changes in how much you produce and consume. Even the slightest bit of effort can greatly increase your wealth.

And that is the first lesson to becoming wealthy. It is also the "**KEY**" to wealth.

Those who understand that resources are scarce, and produce more than they consume will become wealthy very easily. Those who don't, and consume more than they spend will become poor. This will also happen very easily. So remember,

"Resources are scarce!"

THE SEED OF WEALTH

All fortunes start with a seed.

This is a Universal law of wealth. It's no different to planting a garden. You have to place a seed in good soil, in a sunny spot, and water it. And the more often you water it, and allow it to see the sun, the better it will grow.

Anybody who believes otherwise is a **fool**. By now, you should have worked out that the world is full of **fools**. But that doesn't mean that you have to be one.

Would you expect potatoes to grow if you never planted any? Of course not, and neither can you expect to become wealthy if you never plant any seeds in the form of savings.

In order to begin building your wealth, you need to work out where your first seed will come from.

Do you have a job? Are you self-employed? Or are you on welfare? Perhaps you receive a pension? Maybe you just do odd jobs around the neighborhood, or have a service that you can sell? It doesn't really matter. They are all seeds, and each is just as good as the others.

Whatever the case may be, that is where you will start.

It is extremely wise to begin building ones wealth from the very money source that is already available to them. After all, it's just sitting there waiting for you to use it. If you can understand that, you are far smarter than most people.

Too many people stay poor, while fantasizing about wealth appearing from nowhere, while a perfectly good source of wealth was right in front of them, being squandered.
And of course, as with all things, the sooner you start the better. So therefore, you may as well start planting now. It is surprisingly easy.

I want you to list every single source of money that you have, the amount that you receive from those sources and the regularity with which you receive it.

It's not much, is it?

Don't worry. Most people are quite shocked to learn just how little money they make in a year. It's because so much of what they spend is borrowed.

That is the world that we currently live in. And it is also the reason so many people fail to plant a seed of wealth for themselves. By the time they have finished spending, there is nothing left to plant, and they owe what they earn before they even have it in their hands.

BORROWED VERSUS EARNED

Borrowed funds have to be paid back with interest. They will make you very poor over time as you give your creditors far more than they gave you. Earned money does not. It can be invested, to bring you enormous returns as they build in size.

Keep that in the back of your mind. You'll realize the importance of it later.

The only thing that's important now is that this earned money you already have available to you, will be the beginnings of your wealth. It is your seed. All you have to do is plant it.

BUILDING WEALTH FROM SCRATCH

If there is one thing I have learned about wealth over the last decade, it is that it must be grown from such a seed. Just like everything else in nature.

There is no such thing as instant existence. This is also fully testable. You can go out and look in the garden as much as you want, but there will never be plants there unless you plant them.

And that start must be from the money you already earn, and how you use it. That's how I built my wealth, and it is how all the truly rich people I know built their wealth.

Sure, there are people who win lotteries, or are given inheritances. Or find some other easy way to money. But they do not retain their wealth long enough to be considered wealthy. They squander it quickly. Giving it away to people like me through one means or another. They are what I like to call "The Temporary Wealthy."

True wealth is a very different thing.

AMUSING ANECDOTE

My older brother worked for many years in a casino as a croupier. And during that time, he stripped many of these "instant millionaires" of their money within days (sometimes hours) of them winning it. I recommend going in to watch how quickly someone can lose a million dollars in a casino. It's absolutely fascinating!

It also shows you why giving money to people who want to be poor, is a complete waste of time. So if you've been giving to charity, you might want to stop. They're just throwing *your* money away.

But now, it is time to get onto each step in the wealth building process.

Read them carefully, and regularly. Then follow them strictly. If you do, they will bring you much wealth and happiness.

Here's a helpful tip to start.

> *"Nothing comes from nothing."*

STEP 1
PRODUCE AN INCOME

It is a man's responsibility to pay his own way through life. Therefore he must produce an income. There are many ways to take this first step toward wealth.

WORKING FOR OTHERS

You may choose just to take a job of any kind to get started, whether it is in the fields picking fruit, or flipping burgers at a diner. You could even stack shelves in a supermarket. An unskilled job is an unskilled job. It will bring you income without responsibility, and nothing else. Do the work well, and walk away with the paycheck.

Some will choose to take a skilled position. Perhaps you have an IT qualification, or an engineering degree? Or you are lucky enough to be well connected and able to find a management position. These types of qualifications will lead to corporate jobs that pay a higher rate. In some ways this is good. But be cautious not to get too caught up in it, as many people do. Corporations are nasty creatures who would dominate your life if given the chance.

You want to make yourself rich. Not the share-holders of the corporation. Once again, do your job well, and walk away with the paycheck. But when the day is over, go home and get on with building your own wealth. No staying late. For that is a fool's game.

Or you may be involved in a career that you care deeply about. This is the highest paying type of work. Because a person who enjoys what they are doing, will always be better at it. And their employer's will always appreciate their efforts more, and rewards will naturally flow. Enjoy it, and use the money that comes from it wisely by following this book.

By all means, feel free to stay late if you love it.

WHAT IF YOU CAN'T FIND WORK? OR DON'T WANT TO WORK FOR OTHERS?

Then you must use a skill or talent to **create** a job.

Grow fruit and sell it. Create fine art and develop a client base of collectors. Hire out your time as a laborer. Mow lawns for those less physically able. Babysit children. Paint buildings. Buy goods for a low price and sell them for a higher price in a different area. Provide security to a business that cannot afford security guards. Teach a language or skill. These are just a few of the ways, and there are many more.

"Where there is a will, there is a way."

The more time you spend thinking about how to earn, the more ways you will come up with. And whatever you choose, all you require is an income. The source itself is pretty much **irrelevant**. Because it's what you do with that income that matters.

WELFARE RECIPIENTS

If you are on some form of welfare (and it is my experience that **far** too many people are), then you need to find ways to make the best use of this income and the time it allows you to have. For, if you are going to live off the backs of others, you at least owe it to them to make good use of the time and money they provide to you.

Strangely enough, you will quickly find that people will not resent you, if you are doing something productive while on welfare. Even though they are paying for it! And in many cases, they will even go out of their way to help you further.

But they most certainly **will** resent anyone who is just having a holiday at their expense.

YOU CAN BUILD WEALTH ON WELFARE

I have several clients who started on welfare, and have become quite wealthy. So it is definitely possible to do so.

I myself started out on a $125 a week part time job. So it's not your income that matters, but rather how you handle it.

They have followed the rules of this book in the same way a working person would, and have ended up in a position where they were able to get off welfare far faster than most people. They took the attitude that their welfare check **was** their income.

Once you possess income, whatever it may be, the rest is purely formulaic.

STEP 2
SOME OF IT IS YOURS!

A very wise man once said, "How foolish are those who give to others before giving to themselves?" No truer words have ever been spoken.

Do you understand what he meant?

The only way you are going to become wealthy is if you **keep** some of what you earn. After all, how can anyone grow wealthy if they give away every cent as soon as they receive it? And how can anyone be rich if they reject money and throw it away like trash?

The answer is simple. They can't.

This may confuse some people. You may be thinking that all your earnings are yours. But ask yourself this. Are your clothes free? How about your food? What about your home? Or that glass of milk you just drank? In fact, can you think of anything that is free?

You have to pay for it all. And that is why saving is so important, because if you don't pay your-self first, then there will surely be nothing left after paying everyone else. The world is full of vultures who will keep taking till there is **nothing** left.

At this stage, it is unlikely that you are retaining **any** of your earnings.

Most people go their entire lives without ever keeping a **single** dollar of what they have earned over the years. Imagine that. Going your entire lifetime, and dying, without a single dollar to show for it.

That is what must change if you want to become wealthy.

PAY YOURSELF FIRST

The most important step to growing wealth is to understand that you must pay **yourself** first. Before you give away your hard earned money to the endless hoards of people who have their hands out demanding it, you have to set some aside for yourself.

And you have to keep it **forever**.

That money is the reward for **your** efforts. And it will increase your wealth exponentially as it returns interest on whatever you invest it in. And that interest returns interest. And that interest returns its own interest. And so on, and so on.

Wealth is like a living creature. It propagates itself.

This one rule alone will eventually make you very rich, as the interest on your savings will eventually outstrip your income from your employment.

Generally speaking, each dollar you manage to save will eventually return many hundreds of times its own value. So the more you keep, the wealthier you will become.

But that's not the only benefit.

THE MORE YOU KEEP, THE MORE YOU EARN

There is nothing like keeping some of your money for yourself. It will lead you to earn more, and do more with your life.

Sure, at first it is difficult because you have been taught your whole life to reject money, and give it away to others. But after a while, you start getting used to your growing wealth. Then you will start enjoying your wealth.

YOUR LITTLE SECRET

That little secret stash will bring you confidence, as you walk past all the poor people in the street, knowing full well that you are better than them and decidedly richer too.

And the more your wealth builds up, the more you want to keep. This is because your brain is **reprograming** itself for wealth instead of poverty. And this leads to a higher income.

As you keep more for yourself, your brain is rewarding you with long term pleasure. The same way a poor person's brain rewards them with short term pleasure when they spend.

The chemical levels take a while to adjust, but they do eventually.

THE PSYCHOLOGY OF SAVING

As your wealth grows, your dreams will grow with it.

If you currently earn $500 after tax, and keep $50, your mind can't help but feverishly wonder how much you would get to keep if you earned $600. Then it finds way to **earn** that $600. And from there, your brain will find ways to keep increasing your income, as the chemical rewards also increase.

Nothing encourages a man more than keeping some of his income. And pretty soon, he is working out ways to **earn** more, and **reduce** what he pays to others. And with each change in his productivity and consumption, his wealth builds. As does his confidence.

That confidence is actually just a chemical release. Similar to the one you feel after talking to an attractive member of the opposite sex. (Or same sex, depending on your genetics).

EARNING BRINGS PLEASURE

Once a man has gotten out of the habit of feeling pleasure from trivial spending (weak rewards), his brain will rewire itself to feel pleasure from all the things that increasing income and wealth brings (strong rewards).

This is because more income doesn't just bring the satisfaction of more savings. It also increases the other parts of the formula.

He will still have 60% of the higher amount to spend on essentials. And he will also have 10% of the increased amount to spend on luxuries. Not to mention the 20% for paying off debts which will bring him closer to one of the main goals, being debt free.

His entire life improves.

All because he can now see that he will get rewarded for his efforts, and responds in kind by making more effort. It is a natural response.

THE ONLY WAY TO WEALTH IS TO KEEP SOME

So, if you want to be rich, you're going to have to keep some of what you earn. And as you will have seen in the wealthy person's budget, that amount is 10% of what you earn.

This 10% is your seed.

If you think that is too much, ask yourself this. **Why** is it too much?

By all means, it is only right that you pay for the resources you do not produce, but do (or did) consume. But isn't 90% of your income enough?

Is the desire to keep a measly 10% of your earnings for yourself really so bad?

Shouldn't you get to keep **some** of what you worked so many hours of your life for?

Once you agree that you should not have to give **all** of what you earn away to others, you will start on the path to wealth.

WITH TIME AND WISDOM COMES WEALTH

Don't ask me why, but as time goes by, and if you've been following the formula strictly, you start to save more, and spend a lower percentage of your income. It's just one of those weird quirks of life.

Some of this is because the return from your investments is getting so large and can provide you with an amazing life.

Some of it is because you're growing up and realizing what a scam most spending is. You find much more enjoyment in your lifestyle, friends and hobbies than you do in shopping. You find yourself buying land or other assets that create more returns, instead of the latest fashions.   It is not intentional. It just happens.

But you won't worry about it. Because you will find that by that stage, you have some really good friends, and really interesting hobbies that fascinate you. You'll be at a point where you don't have to work for someone else, and nobody has any power over you. And you will travel more, and do more with your precious time.

So, the day will eventually come when you will end up saving most of what you earn, letting it earn you even more money, and living a wonderful life on a small part of that. In other words, you will be wealthy.

Something you once thought was unobtainable.

PLANT THE SEED

The 10% that you keep is the seed of your wealth. From it, and its investment, you will derive interest payments that will build your wealth exponentially. And after a while, you will be able to spend some of these interest payments to improve your lifestyle. It may take a few years, but the day will come.

If you need any further convincing that this is the way to wealth, then consider an example. It is actually based on my own wealth, and the foundations that started it.

Note clearly that I have omitted the false starts in my early years. The example starts from the day I began following the formula **strictly**, and without fail, which is now almost 10 years ago!

MY PERSONAL EXAMPLE

A man (me) who is always broke and heavily in debt ($56,000) earns $20,000 per year after tax, and decides to start following the formula strictly, after a few false starts.

He invests it in a savings account that pays 6%.

After 1 year, the previously broke man has roughly $2120.00 in savings and has reduced his debts by $4000. He is very happy at this result.

After 2 years, he has roughly $4400.00, and has now reduced his debts by $8000. More opportunity has begun to present itself. Several debts are now fully paid.

After 3 years, he has been inspired enough to increase his income to $32,000 and reduce his necessary costs to less than half his income. He now has almost $10,000.00 in savings, and has paid $14,400 from his debts. Only three big debts remain.

After 4 years, he has once again increased his income to $34,000 and has now saved more than $14,000, while decreasing his debts by $17,800.

It was at this point that things **really** took off.

In the fifth year, I almost tripled my income ($92,000). A side business that I did in my spare time became my main income.

I cut back on expenses as much as I could (I lived leaner than I previously thought humanly **possible**), and put the extra into getting out of debt. Expenses were 40%, and debts took 40%. I kept saving 10%, and enjoying 10%.

Those were good days.

From there, it wasn't long till my debts were all fully paid, and I had enough money in the bank to feel completely secure. And things just kept getting better. With no debts left, I was able to boost my savings enormously. I was accomplishing more than at any time in my life, and I loved it. Every day I went to bed feeling like I had achieved something.

Now, I am earning many, many times what I ever thought I could earn. I have found new ways to earn money, and new ways to reduce the percentage I pay to others. Yet strangely, my enjoyment of life is greater than ever. I've taken up a range of hobbies and interests.

And my wealth is now becoming immense.

Here I am, nearing my 10 year anniversary, and the only regret I have is that I did not start sooner. But you can't change the past, only the future.

A CAUTIONARY TALE

This is not just an example of how this formula works. Or why you have to keep some of what you earn. It is also a cautionary tale.

How?

Imagine if I had done what **most** people do, and gone on spending all my money. Buying things I couldn't afford, and investing in "get rich quick" schemes, believing that somehow, it would all just magically work itself out.

Imagine a scenario where I had **not** followed the formula strictly, and had kept nothing of what I earned.

What do you think would have happened?

Right now, at very best, I would still be broke, as well as even more heavily in debt. I would have no savings. And certainly would not be approaching millionaire status. I would owe so much money, that there would be almost no possibility of ever getting out of debt.

I would have lost my properties from the crash of the housing bubble. (Yes, I was once the type of **fool** who believed they could buy property, with little or no money down).

I would only be earning a tiny fraction of what I now earn.

In fact, it is likely that I'd still be making $20,000 a year. Maybe, I'd still be working in the very same humiliating job that I absolutely hated. The wages that came from it would still be going to other people.

My lifestyle would be absolutely awful.

There would be no holidays, no travel, no house or garden. No nothing! In other words, I would be a worthless piece of **shit**. Like most of our society.

But that's the very best outcome. More likely, I would be completely ruined and homeless.

TAKE A LOOK AROUND

Now, I want you to go out for a walk in any city in America and take a look at all the homeless people. That is their reality.

WHICH OUTCOME WOULD YOU PREFER?

I am guessing that you are in a similar position to what I was in 10 years ago. Maybe a little bit better, or maybe a little bit worse. But give or take a few things, your life won't be too far different to what mine once was.

Ask yourself, where will you be 10 years from now?

THE BETTER OPTION

I'm giving you the option to be somewhere better. I'm giving you a formula that will allow you to live as well as I do. And I live very, very well.

All it takes is to start **keeping** some of the money that you earn.

GAME ON

You can follow the formula. Or you can follow those homeless people into despair. It's your choice.

Just understand that your 10 years began when you opened this book.

STEP 3
CONTROL YOUR EXPENSES

Something all truly wealthy people have in common is that they control their expenses.

This is immensely important when it comes to getting started on the road to wealth. Because you will never be wealthy if you have no control over what you spend, or just let others take whatever they want without limit.

Whether it is your necessities or your luxuries, you should always be in total control and know **exactly** how much you are spending, and **where** you are spending it.

WRITE IT DOWN

The best way to measure what your expenses are, is to buy a cheap notebook, or better yet ask someone for a free one, and write down every single expense.

Record every cent you spend like your life depended on it. In many ways, it does.

Carry it around with you for 24 hours a day, 7 days a week and make it the most important part of your existence. And it **is** the most important part, because this is where you get to see what is draining your wealth.

This is where you get your first glimpse of the **truth**.

IDENTIFYING WASTE

You should mark each expense as either a necessity or luxury. And at the end of each week work out how much you have spent on each. Within a month, you will have a very good idea of what your expenses are, and how much money is being wasted.

This is usually the point where people change their lives.

I have yet to meet anyone who isn't absolutely shocked by the amount of money that they spend on small unnecessary luxuries.

It's at this point that they start to understand where all their money is going. And the truth spurs them on to action.

"A dollar here and a dollar there will eventually reach a million."

KNOWLEDGE IS POWER

This term is often misused. But what it actually means is that once you have knowledge of something, you are able to use it to your advantage. And knowing where all your money is going is something that you **really** need to know.

Believe it or not, most people don't have a clue where their money goes. They have absolutely no control whatsoever over their spending. They just give money to anyone who asks for it, whenever they ask for it.

Then they wonder why they are poor?

POOR PEOPLE LACK CONTROL

Most people are poor. You may not be able to see it on the surface, due to the residue of the easy availability of credit, but this statement is true.

The majority of the people around you are stone broke, and often heavily in debt as well. Despite the lies they may tell you, they are all desperate.

That guy driving past in a fancy car bought it on finance. And the people with the overloaded supermarket trolley are paying by credit card. The guy who is buying a round of drinks at the bar is a thief, and the manager who has a nice apartment is committing fraud.

That is the reality of our world.   They are all poor. And they are all poor for a specific reason.

They **cannot** control their spending.

There will come a time in every man's life when he will have to make a decision. He must decide to take control of his spending and be rich or lose control and be poor.

Surprisingly, most choose the latter.

You'd think it would be the opposite way around, but due to sheer **laziness**, it's not. Poverty is not only the easiest path, but also the path most chosen.

The overwhelming majority of humanity is willfully ignorant when it comes to finances and they have absolutely no interest in taking control of their own lives. They want somebody else to be in charge of them.   They want somebody **else** to make the effort.

"Your present is a direct result of your past actions. Your future is a direct result of your present actions."

SPENDING - IS IT REALLY NECESSARY?

You will recall that I told you how most of my clients claim that their "necessities" exceed the 60% they are allowed to spend on them. You will also recall that they were all lying through their teeth. This is the reality of modern day humans. Most of what people consider necessary is nothing of the sort.

Since when was driving a luxury car that you can't afford a necessity? Or for that matter, since when did designer underwear become so necessary either? Or the average of $100 wasted on alcohol and cigarettes each month? How about those brand name shoes?

And as for that air conditioning? You know that people never had that in the past, right?

Most of what you spend goes on items that you could easily live without. And those items are making you poor. You may as well be burning your money in a cave.

At least you'd get some warmth out of it.

YOU NEED TO TAKE CONTROL

Undoubtedly, you will be protesting and insisting that **your** personal expenses are absolutely vital. Stop lying to yourself. The truth shall set you free. As it has a great habit of doing.

Whenever you are trying to decide whether an item is a necessity, ask yourself two questions.

1. Is it food, shelter or clothing?
2. Did people have it a hundred years ago?

If the answer to either of these questions is no, then it is probably not a necessity. It is just a want. And things you just want are not necessities.

DON'T PANIC

Don't worry too much. I'm not asking you to live a life of outright misery. You can have some of your wants, just not all of them. In the formula, you can spend up to 10% of your income on luxuries, but not a penny more. Pick the ones you want the most, and forget the rest.

If you are so desperate to have more, I suggest you start finding ways to earn more income so you can include them in the assigned 10%. Then you will be able to increase the number of luxuries that you enjoy.

The moral of this story is, if you want it, **earn** it!

In the meantime, pick the ones you want the most and buy them. Do without all the rest.

You won't miss them for long. People never do. It's one of the little mysteries of life, that once people can have something, they very often find they no longer really want it.

Most people only seem to want the things that they can't have.

Who knows why? It doesn't matter. Just understand that this is how it is.

HOW TO CONTROL YOUR EXPENSES

Learn to be more sensible!

Most people have absolutely no control over their spending. They just throw money at everything, as if it will fix all their problems in life. Obese people join courses and buy pills and potions instead of exercising. People buy the same clothing and accessories as their favorite celebrities, believing that somehow it will lead them toward becoming a celebrity. In fact, people throw money at just about any issue that comes up. It's their answer to all the world's problems.

But of course, a bottle of useless pills will not help you lose weight, and having the same clothes as a movie star will not make **you** a movie star. Nor will a fancy car make you any more desirable to females. If a girl doesn't like you, it's because she's not interested, and nothing will change that.

*TIP
Your quality of life has absolutely **nothing** to do with how much you spend on it.

EXAMPLE

Take Haiti for an example. This tiny country, with a small population, has been given hundreds of billions of dollars of aid money over the years, yet the people are still dirt poor. Because they do exactly what our people do.

They spend it all on luxuries, and then find themselves broke again. They buy bottled water, instead of digging a well. They hire helicopters to bring in aid, instead of building a road.

They are **spending** instead of **building** their wealth. And just like all people who throw money at a problem, they will get absolutely nowhere.

DEFINE NECESSITIES

Now, let's look at the *real* necessities.

Necessities are exactly that, necessary. Things that you must have for your survival or participation in the society you live in. They include only what you need to have. Such as food, shelter, clothing and any cultural necessities such as a phone or internet access that will give you full access to your society.

SHELTER

Everybody needs somewhere to live. This is very important. What's also important is what you spend on shelter.

RENTING

There are some very simple rules for accommodation. If you are renting, then you want to rent the **cheapest** place possible, while saving the **biggest** deposit possible for your own home. And give away the **lowest** amount of your money you can in the process.
After all, you need to remember that renters are **literally** buying their landlords house for them. And more often than not, they are paying extra so the landlord can engage in a luxurious lifestyle too.

Wouldn't you rather be buying your own home? And paying for your own lifestyle?

*TIP
If you have put aside $150 a week for rent, then try to pay $140 or less. Because every cent you save goes toward your future wealth, and this is how you will grow wealthy. Not by paying $160 and wondering where the extra money will come from.

OWNING

If you are ready to buy, then you want to buy the best house you can comfortably afford, and pay it off as fast as possible. A mortgage free home equals freedom and security.

It is also an asset that you can sell later to provide a high percentage deposit on a better home.

Decide your price range, and spend a lot of time looking at the houses available in that range. Make sure you check out the neighborhood thoroughly for problems, social atmosphere, weather, schools and public transport etc…..

Also, make sure you fully understand the engineering report. **Never** buy a home without an expert checking it over. Those few hundred dollars could save you hundreds of thousands of dollars in the long term.

You don't want to buy a home, and then discover that you are going to have to spend a fortune on repairs, or that your neighbor is a drug dealer.

Do **not** buy a house you cannot afford! I cannot stress this enough, because as many as 2 in 3 people do this. I'll say it again. Do **not** buy a house you cannot afford.

RULE OF THUMB PRICING

Generally, the rule of thumb is to buy a house that is no more than 3 years of your current salary, and pay the largest deposit you possibly can. Every extra dollar of deposit will save you $2 to $4 in repayments depending on the mortgage. If you buy something more expensive, you could find yourself in serious trouble if the repayments go up.

Remember, interest rates do not stay low forever. And we all have decreases in income once in a while. This is an unavoidable part of reality. Shit happens!

People catch a cold, whether they want to or not. And injuries occur every once in a while, no matter how careful you are.

If you're not sure, ask yourself, "Could we afford to keep paying if the monthly repayments go up 20%?" "What about if one of us loses our job, and we have to go 6 months without that income?"

If the answer is no, then you probably shouldn't be buying it.

GET INSURANCE!

Your repayments are not just about how hard you work. They also rely on others. Think about what would happen if your employer caught his wife cheating on him, and they co-own the business. They could break up, and you could lose your job. How would you pay your mortgage then?
Like I said, shit happens. And you need to be prepared for it. Mortgage insurance is a **very** good thing. All insurance is a very good thing. It will give you a safety net, and make sure your creditors get paid if things go wrong. And your creditors **deserve** to be paid. After all, they are giving you their trust.

RENTING VERSUS OWNING

There is no contest. A man who owns his own mortgage free home is relatively safe from the world. No matter **what** happens, he has somewhere to live that cannot be taken away.

But if you rent, you can lose the roof over your head at any moment. The landlord's marriage could break up. Or he might not pay the mortgage. Maybe it is owned by an old lady who signs the property over to her children upon her death, who then get greedy and sell it.

There are even many cases, where the property has been used as collateral for consumer debt, and you find yourself being evicted through no fault of your own.

There are few guarantee's that your rented accommodation will ever be stable.

Renting is a dangerous and very **expensive** game. You are paying the landlord's mortgage, insurance, property taxes, maintenance and other costs too. Usually, they will also be adding on a decent chunk for themselves to **spend** as well.

Most landlords live off their tenants and behave like leaches.

"Greed has no limits. It consumes those it corrupts."

The best advice I can give you, is rent as **cheaply** as you can, for the shortest time possible, and save as much money as you can toward a deposit for your own home. Then pay that home off as **fast** as you can humanly manage.

HOW A MORTGAGE SAVES YOU MONEY

You'd be amazed at how much money in interest payments you can save simply by having an extra percent of deposit, or paying an extra few dollars on your mortgage each month.

Once it is paid off, life becomes a lot easier. You never have to worry about where you are going to live. You are not paying your money to fund someone else's lifestyle. Nor are you buying someone else's home for them.

And all that money you were paying to the bank can now be channeled into the growth of wealth. **Your** wealth! And you have an asset for the payments you made.

DON'T BE CONNED

There are a huge number of landlords out there who like to discourage people from owning their own home. This is for **their** personal financial profit. They use all sorts of techniques, including telling the public that a home is a liability. This is a lie. And if it is such a liability, why do they own homes?

Never believe anyone who claims a home is a liability. They are either lying, or fools, or perhaps a bit of both.

***TIP**

Some people falsely state that renters don't have to pay property tax, repairs etc...Fools! It is *all* included in the rent. Renters are paying for every single cent of it, and usually far more. Your landlord's mortgage is only part of what you are paying. Their lifestyle is the other part.

IMAGINARY DANGERS

People imagine all sorts of dangers when it comes to home ownership. Most of this is due to being misinformed by others who want you to rent forever, and keep paying them forever. But there is nothing dangerous about home ownership.

By all means, it will not be easy, but nothing ever is in life. As with all things, you will have to make the effort, and make the sacrifices required. But as long as you are sensible, you won't have too many problems.

I know that after the credit crunch and the fear mongering lies spread by the media, you may be worrying about foreclosures. There is no need too. Because two types of people lose their homes.

TYPE 1 – FANTASISTS

Those people who bought homes they could not afford, and failed to make their repayments. They are unfortunate examples of how we all get carried away sometimes. In the USA, this was an almost nation-wide phenomenon, and was another symptom of the easy credit boom.

If you are one of those people, learn your lessons and move on with life. Don't drag it out trying to keep a home you cannot afford. You will just create more problems for yourself. And keep in mind that we **all** make mistakes. Use it as a strong reason to act more sensibly next time.

*TIP

If you are honest, and buy an affordable house, and make your repayments on time, you will be perfectly safe. There really is no need to worry about imaginary dangers. The banks are **not** out to get you. They just want their money back plus the interest you owe.

TYPE 2 – SPENDING ADDICTS / THIEVES

These people knowingly bought homes to try and use them as a source of expanding credit or easy profit. As they made mortgage payments (in many cases they didn't), they were re-borrowing the money, and often more on top. They were extending their mortgages, consumer debt, credit cards, and taking second (and occasionally third) mortgages, using the home as security on all of them.

They tried to buy and **flip** properties, then walked away from the mortgage when they could not sell them. As well as deferring taxes (An incredibly despicable act of stealing from the tax payer).

All to get hold of more depreciating money to spend on an unsustainable lifestyle, without any thought of the consequences to our countries future or their children's future.

It is very hard to have sympathy with these people. Personally, I don't, because they really are **scum**.

All I can say is that if you fall into this category, you need to change the way you think about the world. Because you have been **stealing** from the rest of us, as well as your own children, and that is, quite frankly, appalling!

*TIP

If you buy a home to use it as a home, and understand that it is not a credit card, you will not have any problems. But if you are out to **steal** from others, you **deserve** all the misery that comes too you.

HONESTY

Here's another piece of good advice.

Whether you are going to rent or buy a home, be honest! Pay your rent on time. Pay your mortgage on time. And if something happens, tell your landlord/bank manager straight away! Don't sit around hoping for a miracle. They will appreciate your honesty and work with you to find a solution.

And there are always solutions available for anyone who is honest.

CLOTHING

People are staggeringly stupid when it comes to clothing. Instead of thinking about whether the item is good quality, will it last, and will it suit the weather. Not to mention, will it suit the wearer! They worry about which brand name is on it. Or which celebrity wears it.

This should be something that you never consider, because this is just pure marketing, and nothing more. The seller is trying to make you believe something that isn't true.

In this case, they are trying to make you believe that if you wear a certain type of clothing, it will change your life. They want you to be under the misapprehension that by dressing like your favorite movie star, you can **be** your favorite movie star. Or have some kind of special connection to them, which is just complete and absolute **nonsense**, no matter how you look at it.

You'll still be normal old you.

Wearing an over-priced piece of clothing that doesn't fit very well, and doesn't suit you. And it will probably be really uncomfortable too. As for that movie star that you wanted to have a connection with? They still have no idea that you exist.
Grow up! You know that a piece of clothing will not change your life. If you want to change your life, then you need to change your actions. Not the brand name of your clothing!

Currently, the biggest marketing technique is called shepherding, which is to convince people that it is best to be part of the group.

The Nazi's called it "social conditioning". Others call it peer pressure. But those terms are no longer used due to negative connotations. Clothing manufacturers make very good use of this technique.

It involves getting everyone to live the same way and think the same way, and even **dress** the same way, by suggesting that there is one right choice. And that being different, having a different opinion, or wanting a competitor's product is wrong.

It's all about convincing everybody to be part of the "team".

It's based on tribal nature, and is very effective, because humans, by their very nature, don't want to be shunned. And that, of course, goes back to the caveman days where anyone who was shunned by the family group died out very quickly.

Buy clothing that you **like**. Not what someone else tells you to like. By all means, if you love it, buy it. But do so for the right reasons.

Paying $200 for a $20 shirt because it has some idiot's name on it is about the dumbest thing you can do. Not just because it's a waste of money, but also because what may look good on a model, or celebrity is very **unlikely** to look good on you.

For evidence of this, just look at all the overweight women who wear skin tight leggings!

And also for the much simpler reason, that it's still a $20 shirt!

GET YOUR MONEYS WORTH

Better to spend your $200 on a non-brand name item that is worth $200, than $200 on a piece of crap that is only worth $20. So, when you go shopping, look for items that you like, and that make you look good. Get something that is worth the money you are spending.

YOU DON'T HAVE TO WEAR RAGS

I'm not in any way suggesting that you go to extremes and start dressing in rags, because all people should have pride in their appearance. And you will achieve little by looking homeless.

I'm just asking you to buy clothes that give you value for your money, nothing more.

By all means, I'm a big believer in buying high quality clothing, but more often than not, people buy the lowest quality clothes based only on a brand. And this will only end up stripping you of wealth in the long term. And you have to wear inferior clothes because of it.

FORGET THE BRAND

Think about what you want the clothing for, does it suit you, is it a complementary color, do you like it, is it well made? Does it make you look good? These are the types of things you should be asking when shopping for clothes. Not, "Does [insert celebrity] get paid to endorse it?" And they **do** get paid to endorse products!

They get paid a fortune to lure in all those suckers. Remember, this item of clothing was **not** designed by a fashion designer, or sewn by any celebrity. It was designed and made up by minimum wage workers in a factory somewhere, and then just had the designers / celebrities name added to it.

I, and many others, have worked in the fashion industry, and know this for a fact. Many of the top "designers" did nothing more than look at some designs and pick a few to put their name on. And very often, they don't even do that much. That is the dirty little secret of the fashion world. All the work is done by peasants.

Your favorite celebrity / fashion designer did not spend the last 10 years of their lives designing and sewing them all personally. They just exploited some poor slaves in Eastern Europe or Asia, who are likely bordering on starvation.

Always keep that in mind.

BILLS

In today's world, there are many other costs that are also necessities. They are necessities because they are unavoidable, and you are at a massive disadvantage without them. These are called cultural necessities.

Unlike our ancestors, we do not have the privilege of being left alone to enjoy our lives once the work day is over. Nor do many people have the ability to just walk a few minutes down the road to their place of employment anymore.

Corporations now want total access to their employee's, and they locate businesses for their own fraudulent tax breaks and political gains. No matter how inconvenient it is to their employee's.

In government, bureaucracy rules the day, making even the simplest of paperwork difficult. Things that used to be straight forward and easy like getting a passport now require enormous patience, and funds.

Then there is technology.
We live in a **connected** world, and even locating a job is now no longer possible without things like a telephone and internet access. So these are all going to be costs that you have to endure. Whether you like it or not! It is just an unfortunate part of reality that you have to pay a second time for these services, even though your tax dollars built the infrastructure in the first place.

The trick is to minimize them as much as you can.

HOW TO SAVE ON BILLS

You will be amazed at how much you can save on these costs by looking at different options, and packaging everything with one provider. Also, consider alternative options. An example of this is that a roaming service on your mobile phone makes calls prohibitively expensive, yet it is quite cheap to unlock your phone and buy a local SIM card in another country.

You also have options like pre-paid phones, so you can control costs. There are different internet packages, allowing you enough access to stay up to date, but not so much that you end up wasting enormous amounts of time.

Consider all the options available to you. This will help you keep many of these bills down. Remember, you have 60% of your income for your essential expenses, so you want to get the most for your money, and go without as little as possible.

TRUE FACT

Nobody should be paying a single cent for internet use. The inventors gave it away for free, and ISP's already receive numerous tax incentives to make services available. Their charges are **pure** greed.

FREE STUFF YOU HAVE TO PAY FOR

There are many bills for things that used to be free. Like land taxes, water, police checks, medical insurance and a whole host of other things that were once included in your taxes (and should still be), but now come as separate entities.

You need to minimize all of them, because these costs are nothing more than "theft by rule". For those who don't know, theft by rule is when corrupt political leaders change or create laws for their own financial of political benefit.

It's what feudal warlords and the aristocracies used to do in the old days. Curiously enough, this is actually what led to their downfall in the end, which makes me wonder if the same thing will happen all over again. Undoubtedly, time will tell.

By rights, all of these costs are already well paid for in your taxes. And then they have been paid for again through tax incentives, and subsidies. But you are still required to pay for them, yet **again**.

It's not your fault that the government fails to control its own expenses. And it is certainly not your fault that they are corrupt. But sadly, you will have to pay. The law is the law, whether just or not. Your only hope is to pray for society to wake up to what is going on, and remove those leaders from power. But in today's world, that is increasingly unlikely.

PAY YOUR BILLS

Anyway, bills have to be paid, they have to be paid on time, and they have to be properly budgeted for, which is another good reason for you to control your expenses as much as you can, because you want to get as many of these necessities as possible for your money.

*TIP

Paying your bills on time, or even early will save you a lot of money in overdue fee's and discounts that companies provide to people with a strong history of timely payment.

Never leave a bill! If you cannot pay everything on time it is a very good sign that you are spending too much.

FOOD

There are two types of food, "Healthy" and "Unhealthy". Curiously enough, they have a direct correlation to "Cheap" and "Expensive".

Fruit, vegetables and grains are really good for you, and are also really cost effective to purchase. They are ridiculously cheap if you go to a farmers market, and you can even grow your own at almost no cost.

Meat is a bit more expensive, but still very good for you, and you don't need much of it. The healthier you eat, the cheaper it generally is. If you have a balanced diet, you will find yourself spending very little on food.

On the other hand, junk food, processed foods and sweets will slowly kill you, and take all your money away in the process.

Think about that. You are **literally** paying to kill yourself. It's like smoking. Why don't you just go out and give some homeless bum $50 to stab you? You'll achieve the same thing in the end. And you can leave a generous inheritance to your offspring.

It's scary how people know this yet still eat like gluttonous pigs.

ANYTHING IN MODERATION

By all means, anything in moderation, but if you want to be wealthy, you're going to have to start thinking about what you eat, and more importantly, how much it is costing you. Not just in direct **financial** losses. But also in lost opportunity cost too.

Have you ever seen an obese person trying to do physical work? At first, it is amusing. Then it just looks pathetic. And finally, it becomes depressing.

The level of effort you can put into increasing your income will have a direct correlation to how healthy you are. And if you are not physically capable, you won't be financially capable either.

Obese people are lazy people. So you should think very hard about making the effort to get fit. You will find that your efforts translate into your earning capacity as well. Making an effort affects your entire life, not just part of it.

You will spend less, earn more, and have more ability to earn. In other words, there will be a triple benefit to your personal wealth. This is a lesson in how all facets of wealth integrate. When you improve your life in one area, you improve it in all areas.

PACKING TANTRUMS

Whenever I am helping a client arrange their finances, food is always an area that they argue over. They insist that their $300 dollar trolley of groceries is **completely** necessary, and are not particularly interested in lowering the cost. They insist that food is something they will not cut back on. No matter what!

Then I ambush them after they've been shopping.

After their purchase, I take out all the frozen pizzas, sweets, sodas, junk food and other complete crap that is not even close to being essential for life. And do you know what is left?

Not much. Sometimes nothing!

POOR EATERS ARE POOR PEOPLE

This is why they are poor. And usually obese too! They are putting luxuries before necessities, and buying them without thinking about the consequences. The amount of rubbish people consume is shocking, to say the least.

Even worse, many of them have children and are feeding it to them too! That's just downright bad parenting, no matter how you look at it.

The average person I encounter eats far more junk than real food. It's one of the symptoms of a dying society.

When you buy food out of your essential expenses, it should only be essential food. It should include fruits, vegetables, meats, milk, grains, nuts and other healthy items of real food. Not processed junk food, or anything else that you like to snack on.

If you want cheese cakes, hot dogs and soda, then buy them with the 10% that is allotted for luxuries. Because that is what they are, and it will also keep your consumption of them moderate.

Too many people believe that somehow these things are essential to their life, when they are anything but, and more likely killing you if you eat too many of them. The reality is you have just gotten too used to living a life of **unearned** ease and leisure.

You have to change that if you want to be wealthy. The only luxuries you should be enjoying are the ones you have earned, because you will find no satisfaction in anything if you haven't worked for it.

If you want to be wealthy, you need to stop living like a self-indulgent pig, and start living like a human being. This is essential.

FITNESS EQUALS WEALTH

The fitter you are, the better you will feel about yourself. And if you feel good about yourself, you'll make more money. This is just how it is. It's one more little mystery of the Universe. And to make things even better, that time you spend at the gym is time you are **not** spending wandering the shops aimlessly, looking for something to buy.

The point is you should consider getting fit as an essential part of your journey toward wealth.

PERSONAL ANECDOTE

When I first started on the path to wealth in Wellington, New Zealand, I was semi-homeless, paying $50 a week to live in a garage with no floor, no lights, no electricity and no running water. It was just an empty wooden garage, with a mattress on the dirt ground, and holes in the wall. My closet was a suitcase, sitting on top of the mattress to protect it from the mud.

Those were hard days.

I realized that I had to change. So as a start, I joined a 24 hour gym and went twice a day to get fit.

I had all my showers there, using their hot water, and their locker to store my "job interview" clothes. I used their water fountain too, as well as shaving three days a week. And I got super fit over several months through exercise and eating small amounts of good food instead of the rubbish that I usually ate.

I quickly found that a lot of my money had been wasted on junk food. Two tins of tuna a week and vegetables every day was really cheap. My food bill came to less than $12 a week.

So that $125 a week pay check that used to feel so **insufficient**, suddenly ended up paying for my garage, the gym, debts and food, and I still had enough to save $25 a week. The extra $3 went on a treat on Fridays.

1. Rent $50.
2. Gym $10
3. Food $12
4. Debt $25
5. Savings$25

Eating proper food and getting fit helped me out of my troubles. And I even got a full time job through a friend from the gym.

Sadly, when I was working properly again, I stopped following the formula and invested in "property", or more correctly, "property I couldn't afford to invest in". That was my first false start.

STEP 4
GET OUT AND STAY OUT!

Debt is a terrible thing. It has been described as a deep, dark hole that is easy to fall into, but hard to climb out of, because the walls are so steep.

That is a very accurate description of debt, and one that I enjoy using, for debt really is surprisingly easy to fall into, and finding your way out takes a **long** time and a **lot** of effort.

Most people never do, because only the most **determined** have the will to scale its walls and reach the sunlight shining up above.

Most people reading this will be in debt.

It is an unfortunate reality of modern day living that our monetary system has been purposely based around it. If you can be bothered to research the issue, you will find that our currency actually **is** debt. There is no **real** money like gold or silver backing those currencies anymore, therefore making them nothing more than pieces of paper with numbers on. It's an elaborate IOU system, where **nothing** of substance was actually loaned. And that is all it is.

The few elite at the top of the system have devised this plan to ensure that the masses of people below them are easily able to borrow currency to have the things they have not earned, and entrench themselves in interest bearing debt.

The principal repayments wipe out the loan, but the interest payments go to the lender who can then **force** the masses to sell them **real** items for that currency.

The good news is you can get **out** of debt. And once out, there are ways to exchange your excess **imaginary** paper money for real money, in the form of resources such as gold, silver, land and other physical commodities.

But before you can do that, you must confront the truth of your debt, and pay it.

20% WILL CLEAR YOUR DEBTS

This formula allows 20% of your income toward the payment of debts. Not a cent less. If you can comfortably pay more, fine. But never stretch yourself. You also have to pay for your current costs.

Over the centuries, this percentage has turned out to be the most optimal. It gets you out of debt over time, while still allowing you to pay for your necessities, luxuries and to save as well.

Many corrupt "financial managers" will disagree with me. They will say that you should be putting as **much** of your income as possible into getting out of debt. That is simply because they are being very well paid by creditors to say that!

SECRETS UNCOVERED

I discovered this myself in my younger years, when a friend who had gone into that industry revealed their dirty little secret to me during a dinner.

They receive kickbacks (renamed non-disclosed commissions) for every client they can sign to a repayment plan, without the debt being frozen. So the repayments never bring the principal down. You pay and pay, and never **stop** paying. There really is no end to it.

GETTING OUT OF DEBT

There is only one way to get out of debt, and that is to pay those debts off and not take on any more. But there is also a very **particular** way that you have to pay them, or you will find yourself treading water like my friends clients did.

HOW TO REPAY DEBT

1. Stop borrowing!

2. Contact each creditor individually and face up to them.

3. Admit your position, and agree to pay regularly.

4. You **must** have the creditor freeze the debt, so it will not accumulate more interest.

5. If they will not freeze it, then refuse to pay and default on the debt.

6. Give each creditor an equal amount of the 20% assigned until each debt is paid.

7. As smaller debts are covered, divide that portion between the remaining creditors.

8. Once every debt is paid, do **NOT** borrow more.

NOT ONE MORE CENT

This is the most important part of repaying debt. To stop taking on more! It is also the **hardest** part.

Robbing Peter to pay Paul will never get you out of debt. It will just dig you deeper into the hole, and the sides will start caving in and burying you. You must **stop** borrowing.

By all means, if you can get a lower interest consolidation loan from the bank to pay all your debts in full, then do so. But it must be a lower interest rate, and your repayments to the bank must still equal 20% of your income.
You need to have the will power to resist keeping those credit cards and store accounts for "emergencies". You are already in a crisis! This *is* the emergency!

Keep in mind that you will always find reasons to spend **every** dollar you give yourself access too. So in order to prevent spending that credit, you must eliminate it fully. For hotels and car rentals, use either a secured credit card, or debit card.

CONTACT YOUR CREDITORS

These people have given you their trust and loaned you money. The least they deserve is for you to man up and go see them. Preferably face to face if you can. During this meeting, explain to them what you are intending to do. You'd be amazed how reasonable people can be if they see you actually have the **intention** of paying them in full.

SHOW THEM

Show them your income, and how you will set aside 20% to be paid equally to each creditor who freezes their debt, and how long it will take to pay them their full share. They will undoubtedly be angry, and **insist** you pay faster, but you have to keep your head and calmly explain that this is the **only** way you can pay them. And get them to sign a written agreement to **freeze** the debt at that level until it is paid in full, in return for regular payment.

IF THEY REFUSE

If they should refuse to freeze the debt, then you should refuse to pay. This is because the interest being added on will make it impossible to **ever** repay it in full. There is no point in paying wolves that just keep coming back to your door for more.

Remind them that you will already be paying far more than you ever borrowed, so they are still making a good profit from your stupidity. This quite often sways creditors to accept when they **realize** that they are not actually losing anything, and will still be getting far more than if you had paid in cash.

But if no agreement can be struck, then calmly explain that there is no way you can keep paying in such circumstances. You are not their personal ATM. The worst they can do is to go get a court order to make you pay, usually at a much **slower** rate than the one you offered.

*TIP

The unpaid debt will go on your credit record, but keep in mind that from now on you will be buying everything in cash, so your credit rating is no longer that important if most of your debts are paid. This is the **power** of real wealth. Having real money and assets can overcome any obstacle, no matter how hard it may be.

By all means, it could **complicate** your ability to get a mortgage. But you'll be surprised how often it doesn't!

MAKE YOUR PAYMENTS!

There is no purpose in coming to these agreements unless you are actually going to **pay** each portion without excuse.

No matter what else happens, you must keep taking that 20% of your income and assigning it to paying your debts. If not, you will find that you just fall deeper and deeper into the hole. There is no more **time** for excuses.

If your income changes, advise your creditor's immediately, and keep paying 20% of whatever you are earning. You will quickly find yourself being treated with much greater respect if you advise your creditors that you have had a pay rise, and will be increasing your payments to them. It shows them that you *intend* to clear those debts.

In turn, they will report this to credit rating agencies, and your credit score will improve over time. Even with a default or two.

ONE BY ONE, THE DEBTS WILL DISAPPEAR

As each debt is repaid, you must take that portion and divide it up amongst the others. This will increase the speed at which you become debt free, increase the level of respect your creditors have for you, and improve your credit score. You will find yourself feeling very good as debts fall away, paid in full, and you will be one step closer to freedom, as each disappears.

ONCE YOU ARE OUT, STAY OUT

I cannot emphasize this enough. Once you are debt free, *stay* debt free!

No more taking personal loans, credit cards, finance deals, or anything else to buy things you cannot afford. There is no point in struggling for years to get out of debt, just to pile them back on and find your-self in the very same hole further down the track.

ASK YOURSELF SOMETHING

Why would you want to pay more for a product?

Think very carefully about this, because that is exactly what you are doing when you borrow. You are increasing the amount you pay for things by adding interest payments to the purchase. Often doubling, or even **tripling** the cost! That is pretty insane behavior if you bother to ponder it.

ACT LIKE AN ADULT

There will always be things you cannot afford. Grow up and accept that. You are no longer a child.

When people borrow, what they are really doing is **substituting** their parents with credit.

They want someone to buy the toy for them, so they can have things they haven't **earned**. That's excusable when you are 10, but not when you are 25! And certainly not when you are in your thirties or beyond!

I repeat, grow up!

NO, YOU DO NOT DESERVE IT!

I've noticed a deeply disturbing trend of "entitlement" over the last 20 years. This is people's **ridiculous** belief that they automatically "deserve" **anything** they want, for no apparent reason.

You **deserve** what you have **worked** for. Nothing else!

All good things in life are earned, and **paid** for in full. If you buy something on credit, it will quickly lose its shine. Because deep in the back of your mind, you will know that you don't actually own it. Nor do you deserve it. And pretty soon, you will stop using it, or let it get dirty and ruined.

But if you did earn it, you will find yourself cleaning it, and taking good care of it, so it will last a long time. That is because it is yours! It is something you can be proud of.

And that is one of the reasons we live in such a "throw away" society. Much of what people "own" got bought on credit. So they have no respect for it, because they know they don't really own in at all. Deep down, they know that they are losers who don't deserve any of the things they have.

*TIP

If you cannot afford something at the moment, then you don't deserve to have that thing at the moment. As you build more wealth, you will be able to have it later. You have earned something when you can afford it with your **own** money.

STEP 5
VALUE FOR MONEY

A lot of people are under the mistaken belief that it costs a lot to live the good life, and that people live a bad life because it's cheap. This is about as **far** from the truth as you can get.   In fact, it's a downright lie.

Living the life of a poor person is **staggeringly** expensive. The cost of one trip to a takeaway can feed your family for an entire day. And things like cigarettes, alcohol and gambling are ridiculously expensive, with no gain of any kind to be found from them.

Those are just some examples of how people are abusing their finances through the cost of living. And there are many more. So in this chapter, we shall look at how you can improve your lifestyle, and buy better products, while saving a lot of money in the process.

THE HIGH COST OF LOW VALUE

Start by having a quick look around at poor people and the types of things they spend their money on. Or maybe, you should just look at your own expenses. They are probably quite similar.

What you'll see is an endless flow of money to things like smoking, junk food, alcohol, gambling, designer clothing, over-sized TV payments, coffee, gadgets and driving expensive cars that they took on credit. Even their shopping trolleys are different to the shopping trolleys of rich people.

They will be full of fizzy drinks, sweets and frozen pizzas, with few vegetables and fruits in sight.

Why is this bad?

Because it costs an absolute **fortune**! As well as degrading your lifestyle.

Do you think a rich person would walk into a bar every weekend and start ordering drinks at $7 a glass, when it cost less than 10 cents to produce them? Of course not!   It's foolish behavior. They leave that to the idiot's with credit cards who are **pretending** to be rich.

Nor would they shop for their groceries at the local petrol station or convenience store!

If you want to be wealthy, you absolutely **must** get good value for every dollar that you spend.

The more value you get for your money, the more appreciation and satisfaction you will feel. And the quality of your lifestyle will rise in correlation to that. Of course, there are bound to be times you buy a chocolate bar, or a coffee. But just don't do it every day like poor people do.

THE DIFFERENCE BETWEEN SOCIO ECONOMIC GROUPS

There is a clear difference in the social behavior of wealthy people and poor people. And it relates directly to the amount of value they derive from their expenses.   Let's look at the two extremes to emphasize this.

People who live week to week usually go to a pub, bottle store or bar. They over-consume expensive low grade alcohol, cigarettes and other items that scream LOSER.

They are often obese, take very little pride in their appearance, and place a much higher priority on luxuries than necessities. They eat at establishments like McDonald's, KFC and Burger King. These high fat foods are also high in **price** and also scream LOSER equally as loud.

You will also find that the people they associate with do not have a lot of hobbies, and tend to be quite boring individuals. Their lives are limited to excessive drinking, drug use, TV shows and video games etc…

You may be uncomfortable hearing that, but it is completely true. And if you've ever gone to a bar, you know it's true. They are dingy, dull places where the only activity is drinking. The people are unbelievably boring.

Conversations amongst McDonalds customer's tends to revolve around the last episode of "American Idol", or their latest shopping expedition and not much else.

Wealthy people on the other hand, mix with other self-made wealthy people all the time. Like me, they have dinner and drinks at each other's houses. Or they go to a high end restaurant or cafe where they are served high quality food.

They have a range of interests and hobbies, and are generally pretty fun people to be around. An entire evening of fun and entertainment with these interesting people usually costs about $20 - $50, and quite often less. (Try finding an interesting person in a local bar – they don't exist).

Rich people might go out for coffee once a week with their friends, sit down and enjoy it in good company and good conversation. They take their time, and appreciate what they are consuming. They comprehend that this is supposed to be an enjoyable experience. Not to mention a treat.

They certainly don't buy a latte every single day on the way to work, in a paper takeaway cup. Rushing to order their coffee, and having their name screamed out when that order is ready, followed by another rush to get out of the store so the next customer can get in.

Do you see the difference?

One is an enjoyable and relaxing treat, while the other is just an addiction to spending money. They've taken café's and turned them into something that resembles fast food. Coffee is something to be enjoyed. It should not be a conveyor belt experience!

Here are some other things rich people do. And you should take note of them, and ask yourself whether you are also doing these things. Because if a lot of people who are wealthy have a certain habit, then there is a good chance that it is related to their wealth.

VALUE HABITS OF SELF MADE MILLIONAIRES I KNOW

1. They use coupons.
2. They buy items on sale.
3. They make use of free and discounted events.
4. They pay cash, and ask for a cash discount.
5. They pay bills on time, or early to get a discount.
6. They look for lower cost / higher quality alternatives.
7. They make a list before going to the supermarket, and stick to it.

They get value for their money. Do you?

GETTING VALUE FOR YOUR MONEY

If you want to be rich, you also need to start getting value for money. Have you even thought about it before? When was the last time you used a supermarket coupon?

Most people don't. It's a statistical fact.

They are far too busy throwing their money away to worry about whether they are getting something tangible in return for it. All a poor person cares about is spending, as fast as they possibly can, and as much as they can. They have absolutely no interest in getting value for their money, and no interest in keeping any of it.

THE IMPORTANT QUESTIONS

Whenever you spend, you should ask yourself a couple of things.

1. Can I get the same exact same thing at a lower cost elsewhere, and would it be worth the extra time and effort to go there and get it.

2. Is the product of sufficient quality for the price that is being charged?

3. Are there cheaper alternatives that can match the quality of this particular product?

These are all important things to think about. And what's even more important is that you take the **time** to think about them.

IMPULSIVE SPENDING

Impulsive spending is the biggest money waster known to man. That's why supermarkets fill entire isles with chocolates and candies near the entrance and exit. It's why you can buy three bottles of coke for $5. They are trying to entice people into buying things before they have the chance to think about it.

Instead of seeing something and buying it straight away. (Monkey see, monkey want). Go back the next day, or following week even. If you still want it after a week, there is a good chance it is worth buying.

But you'll be amazed at how often you change your mind once you've had ample time to consider the purchase.

Once people start giving themselves that time, they quite often decide against the purchase, because they have had time to weigh the pros and cons, and realized that they don't really want it at all. It's like having a "cool off" period to buy a gun. It stops people from doing something stupid.

Hopefully, you are slightly more intelligent than a monkey. So, use that intelligence and take your time to think about the things you do. And get value for every dollar you spend.

Like a wealthy person would.

SHEER STUPIDITY

There is low value spending, impulsive spending, and then there is just sheer stupidity. And sadly, it is **extremely** common.

Sheer stupidity is where you do things that even a child would know not to do. Like getting your face tattooed, turning an argument into a fist fight, jumping off a cliff, or taking any other ridiculous action that is **obviously** wrong.

In the field of finances, there is an almost endless list of utterly stupid things that people do, preventing them from getting any value for their money. These can include:

1. Buying luxuries before necessities.
2. Over drawing their accounts.
3. Defaulting on automatic payments.
4. Missing rent or mortgage payments.
5. Buying alcohol / cigarettes before groceries.
6. Going on a spending spree as soon as they are paid.
7. Shopping for groceries in convenience stores.

The list just goes on and on, and seems to have no end. Humans really can be utterly **stupid** at times.

But I'd like to focus on one of the more common differences between rich and poor that borders on insanity, and definitely falls into the category of sheer stupidity.

When I worked for the budgeting service, it came up again and again, and seemed to affect nearly **all** the clients. This is the tendency by poor people to over spend on transport, in order to try and impress people.

EXAMPLE

I am constantly told by poor people who are in financial trouble that they are too **good** to travel by public transport, and that they would be too humiliated and embarrassed to use it. They tell me public transport is for **poor** people (consistently failing to see the irony in this).

And of course, they don't want to look poor. Poor people never do.

So, off they go to buy a car (and play the big shot). And it can never be a cheap car that they can afford either. No, that would also make them look **poor**, so they take a much more expensive car on credit instead. And it usually comes with some ridiculously high interest rate financing deal, or perhaps a more moderate bank loan if their credit record allows for it (not much chance of that). I even encountered one complete **idiot** who paid on a credit card, at 55% interest!

And it has to be big, because the bigger your car, the bigger your social status, right? And the financing is available. It's not like they have to pay the $5000 for it up front. Who cares what that $200 a month for 10 years adds up too? (It's actually $24,000 ...for a $5000 car!)

So there they are, with their **big fancy car**, which is now going to cost at least twice what it would have if they had paid cash. And more often than not, it will be considerably **more** than twice the cost. And they are now obligated to also pay insurance on that **big fancy car** too, because that is the law. That is also very expensive, because after all, it is a **big fancy car**.

Then there is fuel. Every time you want to use that **big fancy car**, you have to pay again to fuel it. And of course, you have to park it somewhere too. So you end up paying for ridiculously expensive parking, which borders on extortion in most cities.

So there goes a whole chunk of money just to leave your **big fancy car** somewhere each day. God forbid they park a few streets away and walk the rest of the distance. Because, in their minds, that's what **poor** people do. Not people with **big fancy cars**!

And I won't even go into the opportunity cost of the time they lose sitting in traffic and looking for parking. There go a few more hours of completely non-productive time each week, which could have been used to earn more income. Or that could have been spent going to the gym or enjoying a leisurely breakfast at home. Anything other than waiting in traffic burning very **expensive** fuel!

Now look at a wealthy person. Look at the type of person who follows the formula in this book.

First, they want to maximize their income from working, and decrease the costs of working to the absolute minimum. In other words, they want to get value for their money. So they start by taking public transport, or finding work within walking distance, if it is available and cost effective to do so.

Instead of paying for all the fuel costs of the journey, they are only paying a tiny part of it. That saves a few hundred dollars a year. Even if they own a car at that stage, they will often work out the cost of using it versus the cost of public transport and take the lower option.

This gives them a reliable and low cost way of getting to work. While allowing them time for other pursuits as someone else drives them to their place of employment. Maybe they want to learn a language, or just plan their garden. Well, they can! And they are saving money while they do it.

There is no cost of parking, which saves them another few hundred dollars a year. Do you see why those people are **richer** than you?

If they wish to purchase a car, they save the money for it, and are then able to buy a car they can afford in **cash**. Thereby saving themselves thousands of dollars in interest payments. Usually, they will consider the cost of running this car, and tend to pick the size of vehicle they actually need, irrelevant of **imaginary** social status. Ever notice how rich people don't drive SUVs? A large vehicle screams DEBT.

*TIP

I have never purchased a new car. A second hand one is just as good and you can get great deals buying cars at auction that have been repossessed. They're almost brand new, but a fraction of the cost.

THE RESULT

So there they are, saving money on interest payments, the price of the car, fuel, insurance, parking and any other incidentals like maintenance. That's a lot of money. That's a hell of a lot of money!

Over time, they will move up to more expensive cars, but only as they can afford them, and only when it makes financial sense to own that car. Which is why all the **truly** wealthy people end up driving beautiful, environmentally friendly, fuel efficient European cars, which they paid for in **cash**. And they got a discount for paying cash too!

Meanwhile, their poverty stricken neighbors are running around in an over-priced SUV, which they don't **actually** own, wondering how they are going to make the overdue payment to prevent the repossession of their vehicle.

> "Every dollar spent should bring you more than a dollar of value"

That is just one little example of getting value for money versus sheer stupidity.

QUALITY VERSUS QUANTITY

These are two forces that need to be balanced. When you buy a product, you should be making sure that you are getting something that is good quality, and will do what it is supposed to, and do it for a very long time.

Likewise, you should look at the amount you are getting for your money. Often, you will find that it is only a few cents more to buy a large quantity of something, than a small quantity. This works on the basis that it costs almost nothing to produce the product, and that most of the price is in the mark up for the seller, and the packaging.

And they also work on the basis that poor people want to look rich, and will buy the small "exclusive" size, rather than the large economy size.

RULE OF THUMB

If you have to choose, take quality over quantity for you own use and quantity over quality if you are going to on-sell to others. There are exceptions, such as avoiding smaller packages of products, but usually it will work out well. You want the best for yourself and the cheapest for your customers.

REAL QUALITY VERSUS FAKE QUALITY

Real quality is a very well made item that will last a long time. Fake quality is when an item is very well marketed with a **brand name**.

A smart man will buy real quality, and an idiot will buy the brand name. Thankfully, the world is full of idiot's who are just waiting to give you their money for a "cool" name on a cheap product. So there is plenty of money out there for you to make if you are looking at starting a business selling to them.

EXAMPLE

There are 3 sizes of shower gel. Rip off, bigger rip off and biggest rip off of all. They decrease in size as you go along. And nearly 98% (that's a real figure) of bottles sold are the small and medium size. Nobody other than the odd rich person and a few sensible people seem to want the economy size.

*TIP

Wouldn't it be more cost effective to buy some beautiful little display bottles, and refill them from an economy size bottle of gel that only cost a few cents more? After all, it's exactly the same product.

BETTER VALUE MEANS A BETTER QUALITY OF LIFE

There are many, many ways to save money, but getting value for money is the one that will improve your lifestyle the most. You will find yourself consuming better goods, and more of them, while saving money at the same time. What more could you ask for?

VALUE TIPS

1. Always pay cash whenever possible.
2. Balance quality with quantity. It is better to get a little less of something much better.
3. Check the better brands to compare prices. It might only be a few cents more, or even less than the common brands.
4. Plan your meals for the week, then write a list before you go shopping and stick to it.
5. Eat before you shop. Never shop when you're hungry because you will buy a lot of snack food.
6. If you want a high priced item, wait for a sale.
7. Use a washable cloth and towel for house cleaning, instead of buying paper towels.
8. Use cotton nappies instead of disposables if your doctor says it is OK.
9. Always buy on sale if the product will last till your desired date of use.
10. Always ask for discount if you are paying in cash for a high priced item.

Go online to find **hundreds** of other money saving tips. You will be amazed at some of the coupon sites and how much money they will save you. There are actually clubs of people who tip each other off to savings, and they are well worth joining.

I am a member of almost a dozen of them.

STEP 6
FROM A LITTLE TO A LOT

Wealth is limited to those people who use their money to make more.

This is because wealth is based on resources. If a man grows 10 potatoes, and does not replant any, he can expect to run out very quickly. But if he cuts one up into pieces, and plants those pieces, more potatoes will grow. If he does this consistently, he will continue to reap the benefits.

"You reap what you sow."

Money is just a **resource**. And as with all other resources, there are ways to use a little to grow more. This is called investment.

Hopefully by now, you have worked out that you will get absolutely nothing from wasting your money on poor people's luxuries.

Nobody will pay you to smoke, drink, wear brand name sneakers, or any of the other moronic activities that the public takes part in on a daily basis.

That's what makes them **expenses**. And expenses are **liabilities**. They are outgoing amounts of resources.

Investments on the other hand, create incoming resources through interest and returns. They are **assets**. And assets build your wealth.

If people had sense, they would spend most of their money on assets. Things like land, Gold, Silver, mining shares, commodities and anything else that pays interest or can be sold at a higher price than you bought it for. As a result, they would grow increasingly wealthy.

But as with all things, most people **don't** have any sense.

They are far too busy indulging themselves in hedonistic pleasures. So instead of investing and creating a world of plenty, most of the money has been completely wasted on products and lifestyles that add absolutely nothing to their lives, or humanity as a species.

You need to be different. You need to invest.

MONEY CREATES MONEY

It is very true that anyone who has money to invest will find it easier to make more money. This is due to investing that money for a safe return. And any wealthy person can tell you that this is where most of their wealth actually comes from over time.

Investment and reinvestment are the best way to make money, because they are relatively passive. Someone else is doing all the work, and you just have to fund them, then sit back and collect a share of the profits.

Compare this to earnings, where you have to work hard and get almost nothing in return for your efforts. Which do you think is a better deal?

RULES OF INVESTMENT

Good investment relies on three things. And these are:

1. The safety of the investment.
2. The level of return.
3. The length of time required.

SAFETY

The level of return should always be balanced with the safety of the investment. After all, what good is an investment with a 10% return if there is little or no chance you will ever see it?

Likewise, there is no point in investing in a business, if you can place your money somewhere much safer for a higher interest rate. Or even a slightly lower interest rate in some cases.

So a good stock pick that will return 7%, is still a far worse investment than a term deposit that pays 6%. This is because the term deposit offers you far greater security, and is worth sacrificing the extra percentage point for.

In fact, in order to justify moving up a risk class, they should be offering you at **least** 50% more of what you could get otherwise. So anything less than a 9% year on year **guaranteed** dividend would be a silly move, if you can get a term deposit for 6%.

*TIP

No stock pick will ever return 9% year on year. In fact, you will be lucky to average 3% after all the price falls, fees, management costs, losses and devaluations of the currency.

Stocks are a really **terrible** way to invest in the long term once you actually come to understand the real rate of return.

DON'T LOSE WHAT WAS SO HARD TO COME BY

You need to be very careful when it comes to the safety of your capital. You have taken all the time and effort to save this money, so you don't want to lose it on the foolish delusions of others. And you will be quite surprised by how some of the safer investments actually end up paying better returns than the riskier ones.

Term deposits are a very good example of this. You are given a set rate of return, and whatever happens, you get it.

Whereas, shares in a big technology company may look like they will continue to go through the roof, but crash the following day because some kid in China invented a new microchip, making the old technology obsolete.

Once again, shit happens! So a little bit of safety is a very good thing.

You should seriously consider all the safest options before looking to move up a risk class. And if the risk goes up, so should the returns. Some of the really safe options are:

1. Term Deposits
2. Government Guaranteed Bonds (unless that government runs a high deficit)
3. Inflation Proof Bonds
4. Physical Commodities
5. High Interest Savings Accounts

They all pay **surprisingly** well, if you seek out the best ones. And there are some really good ones out there.

DON'T BE AFRAID TO MAKE DEMANDS. IT'S YOUR MONEY

Don't be afraid of changing banks to get a better deal and more safety, or demanding higher returns for any investment if you feel it is riskier (pull out if you feel it is too risky). This is **your** money that everyone **else** wants to use. They are all living off **your** back.

So you should be the one getting the best deal and the most safety of return. Not the greedy sods that couldn't be bothered saving their own capital, and are trying to **borrow** their way to wealth.

After all, those banks and business people are making a lot of money out of your deposits. You deserve to feel safe, and get a fair share of the profits. I cannot emphasize enough that this is **your** money, not theirs. Keep it as safe as you can!

*TIP

Safety is the number one priority of any wealthy investor. Even before the level of return. It is better to accept a lower rate of return and be sure that you will get it, than to chase a larger return and unexpectedly make someone a gift of your hard earned money.

> *"Better a little caution, than a great regret"*
>
> \- George S Clason
> The Richest Man in Babylon

RETURNS

The whole point of investing is to receive a **return**. In fact, you want the **best** return possible within the parameters of safety.

You would be amazed how many "investors" don't actually understand this. They are investing for any reason but getting a return. From wanting to increase their social status, to pushing a political or social view point, right through to buying shares in a company that a celebrity endorses.

It is stunning how **stupid** the general public can be.

There are a million con artists out there who will try to convince you otherwise.

So, if you're investigating an investment and they start talking about community, social responsibility, hot trends, market tracking, ethics, charity or any other irrelevant thing, you should politely excuse yourself, leave the room and never go back.

If you are putting money into something for any other reason than making a profit, you may as well throw it in the rubbish bin and save yourself some time. The reality is you are going to lose that money.

Investments are for **returns**. Nothing else!

WHAT TYPE OF RETURN SHOULD YOU GET?

You should get the **largest** and **safest** one that you can. If a bank is only offering 2%, go to another bank and then another until you find someone who will give you at least 5%. There are plenty of credit unions that will.

If you have $1000 in a savings account paying 5%, when there is a term deposit at the same bank for 7%, transfer your money into the term deposit. Be proactive in these things, and you will quickly find better returns.

If you have a term deposit that is about to mature, or you have almost saved enough money for another one, and see a competing bank offering a significantly better deal for a term deposit. Use it! Don't feel even the slightest amount of loyalty to any investment. You are there to build **your own** wealth, not theirs!

You have to be very careful about which banks you have accounts with. And look through their returns with a fine toothed comb. You will often find much higher interest accounts hiding in the background that are not heavily advertised. (Banks regularly break the law by only offering certain terms to certain customers).

This is all pretty simple once you start to think about it.

UNDERSTAND GREED AND RETURNS

People are greedy, especially when it comes to money, or more accurately, **your** money.

They want to use your hard earned and hard saved money, to make **themselves** unjustifiably rich. In other words, they are trying to steal your returns!   And they do this by trying to deny you your fair share of the profits.

So you have to fight for them.

LAZY PEOPLE DON'T FIGHT

Never be lazy!

I was always stunned by the amount of clients who were losing out on thousands of dollars every year to avoid taking an hour of their time to open an account with a new bank, or start a term deposit. I struggled to understand how anyone could be that lazy. It was actually quite **repulsive**.

I have also encountered many people who were offered incredible business opportunities or jobs, but did not take them because it **interfered** with their favorite TV show, sport team, or some other ridiculous aspect of their life, like going on a holiday.

Seriously, take a holiday some **other** time!

Then there are the idiot's who bought things on credit card just to avoid walking over to an ATM. Quite frankly, all of these people **deserve** to be poor. And they are.

They were too lazy to follow the formula, and too lazy to get a good return, and too lazy to do anything else that would benefit them. Their doom was self-inflicted.

As you can imagine, none of them ended up wealthy. Every once in a while, one of them will ring up asking for financial help, and I just tell them I'm too busy. There is no point in wasting time with people like that.

I look back with fondness on my time with the budgeting service. It **reminds** me that you can't help anyone who won't help themselves.

GOOD INTEREST VERSUS BAD INTEREST

Interest can either benefit you, or destroy you!

If you are earning it, you will significantly increase your own wealth over time, especially with compounding interest. But if you are paying it, you will merely increase someone else's wealth, as well as eventually go broke. Once again, it is all about simple mathematics.

You want to earn the **HIGHEST** interest rate possible and pay the **LOWEST** interest rate possible.

SUMMARY OF RETURNS

So this can all be summarized by saying, look for the best returns you can, but put safety first.

You will often find that in real terms, the safer investment will actually pay you far more over time anyway. This is because you do not sustain the regular losses that high risk investments come with. And they **all** have losses. So the power of compounding interest is more effective in the long term with safer investments.

Also consider funding yourself. If you have the discipline to follow the formula, chances are that you have many other talents too. Maybe you should be putting your **own** money into your **own** business where you get **all** the returns. It's something worth thinking about.

TIME

As for the length of time you invest, this will always have a great effect on your wealth. The longer you leave money in an investment, the more it will grow, and the faster it will grow. And the earlier you start saving, the more you will have. This is because of compounding interest, or the time effect.

If you put your money in a 5 year term deposit, at 6% per annum, then after the first year, you are earning 6% on your money and the first year's interest. Then after the second year, you are earning 6% on your money, and the first year's interest, and the interest on that interest. And so on and so on. It builds very quickly.

By the time five years comes to a close, you are earning 6% on the initial deposit, the first years interest, the interest on that interest, and the interest on that interest, and the interest on that interest, and the interest on that interest.

And that's just if you put that one amount in, and never save another cent. But of course, you **will** be saving more. You will be saving all the time, adding more and more to the investment.

Go to the next page to see just how effective time is when it comes to investing.

EXAMPLE

Say you earned $18,000 net a year and are lucky enough to be debt free. There would be $5400 in savings after a year, to put in a term deposit. So you deposit that $5400 for a 5 year term.

End of Year 1
$5400 + 6% interest = $5724
+ $5400 from that years savings
= $11,124

End of Year 2
11,124 + 6% interest = $11,791
+ $5400 from that years savings
= $17,191

End of Year 3
$17,191 + 6% interest = $18,222
+ $5400 from that years savings
= $23,622

End of Year 4
$23,622 + 6% interest = $25,040
+ $5400 from that years savings
= $30,440

End of Year 5
$30,440 + 6% = $32,266
+ $5400 from that years savings
= $37,666

In the first five years, assuming no extra income or pay rises of any kind, you have earned over $10,666 of interest on only $27,000 of savings! That's an almost 40% return on your money. That's like getting paid for an extra 7 months at your job during that 5 year period.

IT KEEPS GROWING

At the end of year 10, when you have only saved $54,000 of your own money, you actually have $80,845. An almost 50% return on your money, once again, assuming no extra income or pay rises. This is an extra year and a half's income in practical terms.

Then at the end of year 12, you will be making more money in interest, than you save in a year!

At the end of 20 years, when you have saved $108,000 of your own money, you will have a staggering $215,957. And your next interest payment will amount to $12,957. More than twice the amount you save in a year. You just worked for 20 years, and got paid for 26 years.

Think about that! In 20 years, working the exact same job, with no pay rises, your interest payments have provided you with an extra 6 years of pay that you didn't have to work for.

Now **think** about this:

You **won't** be working the same job. Nor will you be **earning** the same amount of money. Because as the figure in your bank account goes up, so does your desire to earn more.

A man with money behind him is a man with confidence, and he will naturally achieve greater things with his life. He will have increases in his wage, and find ways to make more money on the side.

And equally, more investment opportunities will come his way, paying far more than 6% per year.

INVESTMENTS OVERALL

This brings us to the basic reality of investments. They need to be regular, and they need to be for the long term. The more you save, and the more regularly you save, the sooner you will find yourself in a position where you can live off the interest, and still increase the total in the bank. And it happens faster than most people think.

Theoretically, you should be looking at 30 years, yet most people who follow this formula actually get there in 5 to 15 years.

Imagine that! Imagine a day when you don't have to work for your income. You can earn enough interest to fund your entire lifestyle, and still have interest payments left over to keep your wealth going up. You could spend your time doing better things, like travelling, taking up exotic hobbies, or anything else that your heart might desire. If you are 20 now, you could have it all before you are 35.

It's a nice thought, isn't it? But it is not just a dream. It is **entirely** within your grasp. And this formula will take you there.

At that point, you will be wealthy.

*TIP

Many "smart" stock traders believe they are getting wealthy, only to find that when they add up the fees, losses, currency devaluation and costs of trades, they would have actually been better off placing their money in a term deposit, or other safe investment. It is a source of constant amusement to the truly wealthy.

WHAT INVESTMENTS TO AVOID

Thanks to the nastier side of human nature, there are far more scams than real business opportunities out there. But if you follow the three simple sections we've covered, you will find a safe investment.

It could be a term deposit, or land, or bullion, or commodities. Maybe you'll buy a farm, or open up a small business. Who knows? That comes down to what suits you. All that matters is that they are real, and pay a return. Most importantly, they must be safe.

Scams are usually quite obvious. They will be too good to be true, offer ridiculously high returns, or not make any sense to you. Generally, if you cannot easily understand it, it is a scam.

THE BIGGEST SCAMS

1. Multi-level marketing. Any type of pyramid scheme is a scam at some point. Stay as far away as possible to avoid losing money and friends.
2. Making money online. Despite being featured in an endless array of news warnings and court cases, people continue to fall for these. You will NOT make thousands of dollars a month processing emails, or sending electronic chain letters.
3. Experimental products. You have no idea what will, or won't sell in the future, or even whether they will finish developing it. So leave your psychic abilities at the door, and invest in something you know will sell for sure. At least invest in something that currently exists!
4. Anything religious or spiritual. Selling fantasies to deluded people creates victims. Sure, it may be highly profitable at times, but do you really want to be a conman? Better to be honest and trustworthy. People will respect you more.

5. Franchises. Why are you paying someone for a brand, when you could start your own? Unless it is an amazing deal with good benefits, avoid paying for someone else's brand.
6. Convoluted Ideas. If you don't understand it, don't put a single cent into it. It is undoubtedly a fraud.
7. Buying off the plan. This goes back to buying things that don't exist. Why would you buy something that doesn't exist???? Seriously!!! You have no idea if that builder will actually build the house. And you have absolutely no comeback if they don't.

Of course, there are far more scams out there, but these are the really big ones. Along with anything that promises ridiculously high guaranteed returns like 15% or even 20% per year, without showing how those returns will come. That's a tell-tale sign that you are being conned.

BEWARE OF CONMEN

There are far too many "investments" out there, where people are really just trying to use your money, while giving you as little as possible in return for the use of it. Sometimes, they have no intention of paying you anything.

It's amazing how many "businesses" are really just a group of people **borrowing** money, **spending** it lavishly, then declaring **bankruptcy**. It happens all the time. So you have to protect yourself, and avoid becoming yet another victim of these fraudsters.

WHAT CONSTITUTES A GOOD INVESTMENT?

It's simple. A good investment is one where you can see the very real possibility of a good return, the safety of your capital, and also see exactly how you will take possession of that return.

EXAMPLES

1. Term Deposits. You can see the interest rate you will earn, and also know the exact date you will be paid. They can even tell you how much it will be.
2. Bonds. Once again, you have an exact amount of return and date of return.
3. Arbitrage. You can buy a product at a low price somewhere (wholesaler), and sell elsewhere for a higher price (retail). And if for any reason that sale falls through, you still have a product that you can find a buyer for.
4. Commodities. You produce at a low price and sell at a higher price. This is often the most profitable of all investments, as well as being the easiest to keep direct control of.

There are lots of good investments out there. And they will all benefit you like no other source of income. Just remember the rules, and you won't go too far wrong.

1. The safety of the investment.
2. The level of return.
3. The length of time required.

These are three things that must **never** be violated. No matter what the reason.

The one thing you have to remember when you are investing is that this is **your** money. You worked for it, you sacrificed things to save it, and you want a return on it. Do not allow it to be stolen. Nor should you allow someone to use it without paying you a significant rate of return for that use.

THE VANITY OF BORROWERS

The world is full of "businessmen wannabe's" who think they are so wonderful that you should just be **grateful** for the chance to fund their ideas. They consider themselves incredibly talented and smart. But I'd ask you this, "If they are so smart, why do they need to borrow money in the first place?"

The truth is they are stupid **fools**, like most people. You should only fund them if you can make money doing so. If not, walk away.

> *"Never be afraid to walk away"*

STEP 7
PLAN FOR THE FUTURE

Everybody ages. Everybody dies. This is the reality of life.

The question is whether you **understand** that? Many people do not. They think that they will be young forever and even go to ridiculous lengths to achieve this. But nothing will stop time.

You will go from birth to death, just like everybody else. And your body will age along the way.

This affects you in two ways.

1.   Your lifespan is finite.
2.   You will not always be able to earn an income.

PLAN FOR OLD AGE

Right now, you may be young and fit and completely able to go out and earn a wage. But it will not always be that way. There will come a time when you are physically too frail and unable to work. It happens to all of us eventually.

Even the fittest man in his 70's is not going to be able to do the same things he could do in his 20's. That is a simple reality of life. And naturally, you will not be able to earn the income you used to be able to either.

In fact, unless you have a career that rewards experience, like being a doctor or a scientist, you will start to find it harder and harder to acquire work once you hit your early forties. For **unskilled** people (like me) this will begin at around 30. Older workers are more expensive to hire, and less physically capable. Employers know this.

So how will you pay for things? Have you even **thought** about it?

One of the best parts of following the formula is that it provides for your old age, as well as your own lifelong wealth. By the time you retire, you will be making enough in interest, and own enough assets to not have to worry about it.

This is a much better position than most old people find themselves in when they retire!

*TIP

Every year, the number of elderly people committing suicide goes up, not out of pain or suffering, but because they have literally run out of money and have no way to live a dignified life. That's pretty scary isn't it?

What's even ***scarier*** is that if you don't follow the formula, you're probably going to be one of them.

FORGET A PENSION!

Like it or not, there will be no government pension for anyone currently under the age of 45. This is an absolute mathematical certainty. No matter how much politicians might lie to get votes. The money just doesn't exist.

There are far more people who require government assistance ***now*** than there are people contributing to the system, which makes it all completely unsustainable.

Especially when it comes to government funded pensions. We've gone from a ratio of 16:1 workers to retiree's, to 3:1. And it's only going to get worse. Eventually, we will reach a reversal.

We will be lucky if current forms of governments actually **survive** the next few decades, with the economic mess that we are in. But welfare is definitely on the way out, unless they can find some way to magically wipe out 90% of the human population. But that seems pretty unlikely. The end of pensions is a much safer bet.

Although, you have to put that into context, because most countries never offered their people a pension, and even in the west, they are a relatively new phenomenon, so the west is really just moving back to a state of normality where people have to fund their own old age.

Pensions were a failed experiment in National Socialism, and a very costly failure at that.

PENSIONS WILL GO THE WAY OF BETA

If you are too young to remember **what** Beta was, they were a type of video tape that lost out in a sales war to the superior VHS video tape. If you are too young to remember **what** video tapes were? You can look it up online under the 1980's.

RELY ON YOURSELF

The point is, if you were relying on someone else paying your way in old age, you can forget about it. It's simply not going to happen. You are on your own.

The next generation is not going to pay 75% or **more** in income tax, just because you were too irresponsible to save for your old age. After all, they will already be paying enormous levels of tax to cover all the other entitlement programs previous generations had.

The only money you will have access too, is the money that you saved and invested for a return.

YOUR CHILDREN WILL NOT SUPPORT YOU

You might think that you'll be OK and that your children will take care of you. Like all good children should. But pay close attention to those children.

Do you notice how selfish and self-centered they are now?

See how fast they flitter away their money on any fad that comes along? What about that distinct lack of consideration for others? And how often do they seem to feel "entitled" to things, and extremely **hesitant** to do any real work?

Now, do you **really** think they will take good care of you in your old age?

Or is it more likely that they will come and see you on holidays, and when they want something. That you will find they just consider you a free babysitter and only visit when they want a free place to stay. It is an **uncomfortable** suggestion, I know, but this is the reality of most people's children.

Whether you like it or not, your children are not **you**.

Although **you** may have the desire to be wealthy and make the most of your life, that doesn't mean **they** will. Chances are they will be part of the overwhelming majority of people who like to be poor and think far more of spending than saving. And that means they won't have the funds to take care of an elderly parent.

So you should probably not rely on them in your old age.

*If yours are different, pat yourself on the back. You have obviously been a far better parent than most of our society. And I truly do commend you on that. If only more parents could say the same thing.

FOLLOW THE FORMULA

That is why it is **essential** that you follow this formula, and start developing your own assets and investments, so that you do not have to rely on the charity of others when you grow old.

You want to have the dignity and security of not having to worry about money when you get into your old age. After all, retirement is supposed to be a peaceful and happy time of your life. You should be able to enjoy it.

It's a time to go travelling, have a nice garden and indulge in some rather frivolous luxuries that you can't have when you are younger.

The formula will allow for this.

FIND SECURITY

The more you follow the formula, the more you will be able to make of your life, and the more security you will have for your old age. Your goal should be to own a mortgage free house, and grow enough food that you never have to worry about homelessness, or starving.

Then you should have enough assets to ensure that you can live a nice lifestyle, and those assets should be a mixture of currency, land, housing, commodities, bullion and other solid monies that you can use to guarantee a nice life.

You want assets that will keep bringing you a regular income, or increase in value and be viable to sell. That is the only way that you will be able to enjoy a nice retirement.

They will guarantee your security.

MONETARY SYSTEMS FALL

Don't just rely on cash in the bank, because inflation could wipe that out. It has happened many times in the past, and will happen again in the future. So make sure you have other forms of money as well. If you see one currency failing, then diverge into another currency.

If you own a few rental properties, you can charge in whatever currency is **currently** being used, without too much worry. Food and other commodities are also a good way to make money in your retirement years.

You should also strongly consider learning skills like preserving and jam making. There are thousands of elderly people out there who **survive** off the income these bring. And they are always handy to know, whether for revenue or just personal **enjoyment**.

THIS IS YOUR LIFE

This is the conclusion of the book. After all, I did promise myself that it would be short.

By the way, congratulations on making it all the way through, because my research shows very clearly that most readers will not. Only about 1 in 10 will read it all, and of them, only about another 1 in 10 will go on to follow the formula. And of them, only about another 1 in 10 will follow it strictly and stick with it. So 1 out of every 1000 readers will become wealthy.

The rest were all looking for a free hand out, and did not like the idea of having to build their own wealth.

They will *regret* that in years to come.

Then there are all the people who didn't buy this book to begin with…….

YOU ARE SPECIAL

If you are one of the ones who will go on to wealth, you are very different to the majority of human society.

You have the true desire to be wealthy.

WILL IT WORK?

Yes! This formula works incredibly well for anyone who will follow it. And if you are one of those people, you will have many years of happiness and satisfaction ahead of you.

Sure, there will be times that it is hard and you will wonder if it is all going to be worth it in the end. But then there will be far more times when you realize that it was.

It's all up to you now.

THIS IS YOUR LIFE, YOU ONLY GET ONE

In the short time that you spend in this world, you can be rich or poor, slim or fat, fit or unfit, intelligent or ignorant, happy or sad. It is purely about deciding how you want to live. It really is that **simple**, and wealth is no different. It is also **simple**.

BECOME A GREAT PERSON

Believe it or not, all the greatest people in history were absolutely no different to you. They just made the **effort**. And that is why history remembers them. Because they were productive, and worked hard, and had the attitude that they could do the things they wanted.

And so can you.

The only thing stopping you is yourself.

THE UNIVERSE IS AN EXPERIMENT

Life is one big experiment. And we are all just formulas inside formulas.

We are all mathematical equations in a biological form. No matter how you look at it, every single aspect of life is based on mathematics. Wealth is absolutely no different. Each time the equation inputs are changed, a different result occurs. And you, like any scientist, should be looking for the best result.

And in this case, the scientists who came before you have given you most of the answer. All you need to do is tweak it to your best advantage.

IS THERE A GOD

Who knows, maybe there is some experimenter out there who created us. And perhaps it is looking for the most successful outcomes in its own experiment. But who cares?

Whether there is or not doesn't matter. What matters is that you alter your input until it gives you a satisfactory output. That is the only thing **you** need to be concerned about.

And if it turns out that there is a god. Then that god will be very pleased that you maximized the return on their investment. You will be one of their success stories.

Maybe they will design an entire species based on you. It's somewhat irrelevant.

Either way, you win.

FORGET THE EXCUSES

For any excuse makers out there, who say things like, "What about people in Africa"? Well, there are a lot of **really** rich people in Africa. Many of them have read earlier versions of this book. Like you, they are people who wanted things to be better and found a way to make it so.

And like them, you can walk away from your own bad situation, and change the equation, at any moment you choose.

Whether it is an unloving family, financial irresponsibility, a violent partner, an insane religion or any of the other nasty things that are out there, you can walk away. You are the only one with the power to do so.

They have absolutely **no** power over you if you do not give them any. Change the input, change the result!

This is your life, and it is up to you to use it.

BUILD YOUR WEALTH NOW

Don't wait for anyone, or anything. Because every minute you lose is a minute you will never get back. Forget the naysayers, and the others who say it cannot be done, because it can.

I have done it, and so have many other people.

Decide all the things that you want to get out of life, and go start getting them. They are yours for the taking!

You will find yourself constantly getting ahead, bit by bit, as the years go by. And you will find that you eventually become **far wealthier** than you would have done otherwise.

I wish you the best of luck,
Andrew Costello.

Printed in Great Britain
by Amazon